Michael Field

Sight and song
1892

with

Underneath
the bough
1893

Woodstock Books
Oxford and New York
1993

This edition first published 1993 by
Woodstock Books
Spelsbury House, Spelsbury, Oxford OX7 3JR
and
Woodstock Books
387 Park Avenue South
New York, NY 10016-8810

ISBN 1 85477 143 4
Reproduced by permission from copies in the London
Library, St James's Square, London
New matter copyright © Woodstock Books 1993

British Library Cataloguing-in-Publication Data
A catalogue record for this book is
available from the British Library

Library of Congress Cataloging-in-Publication Data
Field, Michael.
    [Sight and song]
    Sight and song; with, Underneath the bough / Michael
Field.
        p. cm. — (Decadents, symbolists, anti-decadents)
    ISBN 1-85477-143-4: $55.00
I. Field, Michael. Underneath the bough. 1993.   II. Title.
III. Title: Underneath the bough.   IV. Series.
PR4699.F5S5   1993
821'.8—dc20   93–25721
                                                                              CIP

Printed and bound in Great Britain by
Smith Settle
Otley, West Yorkshire LS21 3JP

Decadents, Symbolists, Anti-decadents

Poetry of the 1890s

A series of facsimile reprints chosen and introduced by
R.K.R.THORNTON AND IAN SMALL

Introduction

On the day of the funeral of Edith Emma Cooper (b. 1862), who died of cancer in 1913, her aunt Katharine Harris Bradley (b. 1846) collapsed; she had concealed that she too had cancer, of which she died nine months later. If few had heard of these two women under those names, the world of literature had been aware of the name under which they wrote poems and fiery, extravagant plays, 'Michael Field'. Their output of original work included twenty seven tragedies (they were planning but never completed a comedy), eight books of verse, and many diaries from which a selection was published in 1933. Although one could not say that their work was at the centre of literary life during their active period, they were very much in touch with what was going on and have left a lively record of many of the major and minor figures of the day.

Katharine Bradley was born in Birmingham, the daughter of a tobacco manufacturer. Her elder sister married James Cooper, moved to Kenilworth and had a daughter, Edith Emma. The death of Katharine's father, the joining of the two families and the fact that the birth of a second child to Katharine's sister left her an invalid, threw together the aunt and niece in what was to prove a lifelong pursuit of education, art and literature which was made possible by the family's private means. Katharine attended courses at Newnham and the Collège de France in Paris. In 1878 both women attended classes in classics and philosophy at Bristol University. They were fair latinists, knew considerable German, French and Italian, and Katharine had studied Greek. The poem 'Prologue' in *Underneath the bough* records their defiance of convention and their dedication to literature and to each other, vowing 'Against the world, to be / Poets and lovers evermore'.

Katharine had published one book of verse under the pseudonym 'Arran Leigh' in 1875. In 1881 they published together *Bellerophôn* under the names Arran and Isla Leigh. In 1884 the publication of two dramas, *Callirrhoë and Fair Rosamund*, had a single signature, that of 'Michael Field', as if to indicate the complete integration of the two authors. It was meant to protect them from prejudices against dual authorship but even more from prejudices against female authorship. 'We have many things to say' they wrote to Robert Browning, 'that the world will not tolerate from a woman's lips. We must be free as dramatists to work out in the open air of nature – exposed to her vicissitudes, witnessing her terrors: we cannot be stifled in drawing-room conventionalities' (*Works and days*, p.6). The good reception of *Callirrhoë* made harder to bear the general neglect of their later work, but their habit of publishing in finely-produced limited editions (often at their own expense) cannot have helped to achieve a wide circulation.

They had some success in the avant-garde dramatic circles of the 1890s when their tragedy *A question of memory* opened the 1893 season of the Independent Theatre with Wilde, William Archer and John Gray in the audience; but it did not receive enthusiastic reviews. Indeed Lionel Johnson differed from most critics in preferring the tragedies to the lyrics, as he wrote in notes which he gave to Katharine Tynan in about 1896:

Alone of the younger poets aims at tragedy above all other forms of poetry: the lyrics are well enough, but the play is the thing. An imaginative grasp of historic tragedy, the clash of high passions and forces, the sense of destiny at work. Vigorous language, sometimes over-Elizabethan, but never flat and tame. The earlier work the best: is becoming too subtle and eccentric, less broad and strong. Not afraid of attempting great work: no mincing delicacy, in the prevailing fashion. The plays are *dramatic*, moving, urgent: some scenes of extraordinary force, others of extraordinary grace. In a way, like Mrs Browning: ambitious, vehement, sometimes turbid and turgid and strained, but at least enamoured of strength and largeness. (*Dublin Review*, October 1907, p.338)

Their lyrics and diaries, which are now more highly regarded, contain the same passions but in more elegant structures. In 1889 *Long ago* (in an edition of 100 copies) audaciously attempted to extend Sappho's fragments into lyrics which offered a new openness in the language of desire, and particularly desire between women. In the early 1890s they journeyed around Europe, researching in art-galleries for material for *Sight and song* (1892 in an edition of 400 copies), a book in which they aimed to 'translate into verse what the lines and colours of certain chosen pictures sing in themselves' and which reflects the 1890s willingness to agree with Pater that 'all art constantly aspires towards the condition of music'. Pater is obviously there behind the version of the Mona Lisa, and Flaubert also helped to shape the skilfully vivid pictures; but at the same time, the sensuous physicality of the pictures is expressed in a way which draws, as Angela Leighton says, 'on the adventurous and permissively sensual experiences of their own lives together'.

Retreating from that experiment in publishing with Mathews and Lane, they brought out their next book of poems again with Bell and again in a limited edition of 150 copies. *Underneath the bough*, whose title from *The Rubaiyat of Omar Khayyam* suggests hedonistic indulgence, was the book which most impressed their contemporaries, coming out in a new and reduced edition later in the same year and being pirated by Mosher in 1898. It continues that exploration of free acknowledgement of pleasure and sensuality for their own sake.

   Not achieving even the minor success of the poetry in drama, with the new century their energy began to wane. The crisis brought about by the death in 1906 of their chow dog appears as extravagant now as it did to their friends then; but it did seem to symbolise their pagan sensuality. In its place they turned to Roman Catholicism and a new subject for their poems; but the drive was largely gone with the sensuality. Their poems at their best, however, passionate and pagan, had indicated a new freedom for women to admit, enjoy and express their sexuality, and their significance has yet to be fully explored.

R. K. R. T.
I. S.

Select Bibliography

Primary works (listed chronologically, but omitting the dramas; all books by 'Michael Field' unless otherwise stated)

The new Minnesinger and other poems, by Arran Leigh [pseudonym of Katherine Harris Bradley], 1875.

Bellerophôn [and other poems], by Arran and Isla Leigh [pseudonyms of Katharine Harris Bradley and Edith Emma Cooper], 1881.

Long ago, 1889.

Sight and song, 1892.

Underneath the bough, 1893; revised and decreased edition, 1893; another edition, Portland, Maine, 1898.

Wild honey from various thyme, 1908.

Poems of adoration, 1912.

Mystic trees, 1913.

Whym Chow, flame of love, 1914.

Dedicated: an early work of Michael Field, 1914.

A selection from the poems of Michael Field, compiled by T. Sturge Moore, 1923.

The Wattlefold, unpublished poems by Michael Field collected by Emily C. Fortey, Oxford, 1930.

Works and days, from the journal of Michael Field, edited by T. and D. C. Sturge Moore, 1933.

Useful works to consult

Mary Sturgeon, *Michael Field*, 1922.

Charles S. Ricketts, *Michael Field*, Edinburgh, 1976.

Christine White, '"Poets and lovers evermore": interpreting female love in the poetry and journals of Michael Field', *Textual Practice*, 4 (1990).

Angela Leighton, *Victorian women poets: writing against the heart*, 1992.

SIGHT AND SONG

*** *Four hundred copies only of this edition printed*

SIGHT AND SONG WRITTEN
BY MICHAEL FIELD

ELKIN MATHEWS
AND JOHN LANE
AT THE SIGN OF
THE BODLEY HEAD
IN VIGO STREET
LONDON 1892

ὅσ' ἂν λέγωμεν πάνθ' ὁρῶντα λέξομεν.

SOPHOCLES, *Œdipus Coloneus.*

'I see and sing, by my own eyes inspired.'

KEATS, *Ode to Psyche.*

PREFACE

THE aim of this little volume is, as far as may be, to translate into verse what the lines and colours of certain chosen pictures sing in themselves; to express not so much what these pictures are to the poet, but rather what poetry they objectively incarnate. Such an attempt demands patient, continuous sight as pure as the gazer can refine it of theory, fancies, or his mere subjective enjoyment.

'Il faut, par un effort d'esprit, se transporter dans les personnages et non les attirer à soi.' For *personnages* substitute *peintures*, and this sentence from Gustave Flaubert's 'Correspondence' resumes the method of art-study from which these poems arose.

PREFACE

Not even 'le grand Gustave' could ultimately illude himself as a formative power in his work— not after the pain of a lifetime directed to no other end. Yet the effort to see things from their own centre, by suppressing the habitual centralisation of the visible in ourselves, is a process by which we eliminate our idiosyncrasies and obtain an impression clearer, less passive, more intimate.

When such effort has been made, honestly and with persistence, even then the inevitable force of individuality must still have play and a temperament mould the purified impression :—

> 'When your eyes have done their part,
> Thought must length it in the heart.'

M. F.

February 15, 1892.

TABLE OF POEMS

vii

TABLE OF POEMS

TABLE OF POEMS

ix

L'INDIFFÉRENT

WATTEAU

The Louvre

HE dances on a toe
As light as Mercury's :
Sweet herald, give thy message ! No,
He dances on ; the world is his,
The sunshine and his wingy hat ;
His eyes are round
Beneath the brim :
To merely dance where he is found
Is fate to him
And he was born for that.

He dances in a cloak
Of vermeil and of blue :

A

L'INDIFFÉRENT

Gay youngster, underneath the oak,

Come, laugh and love! In vain we woo;

He is a human butterfly;—

    No soul, no kiss,

    No glance nor joy!

Though old enough for manhood's bliss,

    He is a boy,

  Who dances and must die.

VENUS, MERCURY AND CUPID

CORREGGIO

The National Gallery

HERE we have the lovely masque
    Of a Venus, in the braid
Of bright oak-boughs, come to ask
    Hermes will he give a task
To the little lad beside her,
Who half hides and half doth guide her.

Can there be indeed good cause
    Cupid should learn other art
Than his mother's gracious laws?
    Hermes—Oh, the magic straws
In his hat!—as one that pineth,
To the pretty babe inclineth.

3

VENUS, MERCURY AND CUPID

Oh, the poignant hour serene,
   When sweet Love that is a child,
When sweet Cupid comes between
    Troubled lovers as a screen,
And the scolding and beseeching
Are just turned to infant-teaching.

DRAWING OF ROSES AND VIOLETS

LEONARDO DA VINCI

The Accademia of Venice

LEONARDO saw the spring
　　　　Centuries ago,
Saw the spring and loved it in its flowers—
　　　　Violet, rose:
　　　　One that grows
Mystic, shining on the tufted bowers,
And burns its incense to the summer hours;
　　　　And one that hiding low,
　　　　Half-face, half-wing,
　　　　With shaded wiles
　　　　Hides and yet smiles.

DRAWING OF ROSES AND VIOLETS

Leonardo drew the blooms
      On an April day :
How his subtle pencil loved its toil,
      Loved to draw !
      For he saw
In the rose's amorous, open coil
Women's placid temples that would foil
      Hearts in the luring way
      That checks and dooms
      Men with reserve
      Of limpid curve.

Leonardo loved the still
      Violet as it blows,
Plucked it from the darkness of its leaves,
      Where it shoots
      From wet roots ;
Found in it the precious smile that weaves
Sweetness round Madonna's mouth and heaves

DRAWING OF ROSES AND VIOLETS

> Her secret lips, then goes,
> At its fine will,
> About her face
> He loved to trace.

Leonardo drew in spring,
> Restless spring gone by,
Flowers he chose should never after fade
> For the wealth
> Of strange stealth
In the rose, the violet's half-displayed,
Mysterious smile within the petals' shade
> That season did not die,
> Like everything,
> Of ruin's blight
> And April's flight.

LA GIOCONDA

LEONARDO DA VINCI

The Louvre

HISTORIC, side-long, implicating eyes ;
A smile of velvet's lustre on the cheek ;
Calm lips the smile leads upward ; hand that lies
Glowing and soft, the patience in its rest
Of cruelty that waits and doth not seek
For prey ; a dusky forehead and a breast
Where twilight touches ripeness amorously :
Behind her, crystal rocks, a sea and skies
Of evanescent blue on cloud and creek ;
Landscape that shines suppressive of its zest
For those vicissitudes by which men die.

8

THE FAUN'S PUNISHMENT

CORREGGIO

The Louvre

WHAT has the tortured, old Faun been doing ?
     What was his impious sin,
That the Maenads have ceased from pursuing
     Cattle, with leaps and din,
     To compass him round,
     On woodland ground,
     With cords and faces dire,—
     Cords fastened with strain,
     Faces hate-stretched ?
     Why have they fetched
Snakes from the grass, with swift tongues of fire,
And a reed from the stream-sodden plain ?

THE FAUN'S PUNISHMENT

Beneath the sun's and the oak-leaves' flicker,

       They settle near—ah, near!

One blows her reed, as dry as a wicker,

       Into the old Faun's ear;

       The scream of the wind,

       With flood combined,

       Rolls on his simple sense:

       It is anguish heard,

       For quietness splits

       Within; and fits

Of gale and surge are a fierce offence

To him who knows but the breeze or bird.

One sits with fanciful eyes beside him;

       Malice and wonder mix

In her glance at the victim—woe betide him,

       When once her snakes transfix

       His side! Ere they dart,

       With backward start

THE FAUN'S PUNISHMENT

She waits their rigid pause;
And with comely stoop
One maid, elate
With horror, hate
And triumph, up from his ankle draws
The skin away in a clinging loop.

Before the women a boy-faun dances,
Grapes and stem at his chin,—
Mouth of red the red grape-bunch enhances
Ere it is sucked within
By the juicy lips,
Free as the tips
Of tendrils in their curve;
And his flaccid cheek,
Mid mirthful heaves
And ripples, weaves
A guiltless smile that might almost serve
For the vines themselves in vintage-week.

11

THE FAUN'S PUNISHMENT

What meaning is here, or what mystery,
    What fate, and for what crime?
Why so fearful this silvan history
    Of a far summer-time?
    There was no ill-will
    That day until
    With fun the grey-beard shook
    At the Maenads' torn,
    Spread hair, their brave,
    Tumultuous wave
Dancing ; and women will never brook
Mirth at their folly, O doomed, old Faun!

THE BIRTH OF VENUS

SANDRO BOTTICELLI

The Uffizi

FRILLS of brimming wavelets lap
Round a shell that is a boat ;
Roses fly like birds and float
Down the crisp air ; garments flap :
Midmost of the breeze, with locks
In possession of the wind,
Coiling hair in loosened shocks,
Sways a girl who seeks to bind
New-born beauty with a tress
Gold about her nakedness.

And her chilled, wan body sweet
Greets the ruffled cloak of rose,

THE BIRTH OF VENUS

Daisy-stitched, that Flora throws
Toward her ere she set her feet
On the green verge of the world:
Flora, with the corn-flower dressed,
Round her neck a rose-spray curled
Flowerless, wild-rose at her breast,
To her goddess hastes to bring
The wide chiton of the spring.

While from ocean, breathing hard,
With sole pressure toward the bay,—
Olive raiment, pinions grey
By clipt rose-stems thinly starred,
Zephyrus and Boreas pass,
One in wonder, one desire:
And the cool sea's dawnlit mass
Boreas' foot has lifted higher,
As he blows the shell to land,
Where the reed invades the sand.

14

THE BIRTH OF VENUS

She who treads the rocking shell—
Tearful shadow in her eyes
Of reluctant sympathies,
On her mouth a pause, a spell,
Candour far too lone to speak
And no knowledge on her brows;
Virgin stranger, come to seek
Covert of strong orange-boughs
By the sea-wind scarcely moved,—
She is Love that hath not loved.

ANTIOPE

CORREGGIO

The Louvre

NOONTIDE's whiteness of full sun
    Illumes her sleep;
Its heat is on her limbs and one
    White arm with sweep
Of languor falls around her head:
She cuddles on the lap of earth;
    While almost dead
Asleep, forgetful of his mirth,
A dimpled Cupid at her side
    Sprawls satisfied.

16

ANTIOPE

Conquered, weary with the light,
    Her eyelids orb :
Summer's plenitude of might
    Her lips absorb,—
Uplifted to the burning air
And with repletion fallen apart.
    Her form is bare,
But her doe-skin binds each dart
Of her woodland armory,
    Laid idle by.

She is curled beyond the rim
    Of oaks that slide
Their lowest branches, long and slim,
    Close to her side ;
Their foliage touches her with lobes
Half-gay, half-shadowed, green and brown :
    Her white throat globes,
Thrown backward, and her breasts sink down

ANTIOPE

With the supineness of her sleep,
    Leaf-fringed and deep.

Where her hand has curved to slip
    Across a bough,
Fledged Cupid's slumberous fingers grip
    The turf and how
Close to his chin he hugs her cloak!
His torch reversed trails on the ground
    With feeble smoke;
For in noon's chastity profound,
In the blank glare of mid-day skies,
    Love's flambeau dies.

But the sleepers are not left
    To breathe alone;
A god is by with hoofs deep-cleft,
    Legs overgrown

ANTIOPE

With a rough pelt and body strong :
Yet must the head and piercing eyes
    In truth belong
To some Olympian in disguise ;
From lawless shape or mien unkempt
    They are exempt.

Zeus, beneath these oaken boughs,
    As satyr keeps
His watch above the woman's brows
    And backward sweeps
Her cloak to flood her with the noon ;
Curious and fond, yet by a clear
    Joy in the boon
Of beauty franchised—beauty dear
To him as to a tree's bent mass
    The sunny grass.

TREADING THE PRESS

BENOZZO GOZZOLI

The Campo Santo at Pisa

FROM the trellis hang the grapes
    Purple-deep ;
Maidens with white, curving napes
    And coiled hair backward leap,
As they catch the fruit, mid laughter,
Cut from every silvan rafter.

Baskets, over-filled with fruit,
    From their heads
Down into the press they shoot
    A white-clad peasant treads,
Firmly crimson circles smashing
Into must with his feet's thrashing.

20

TREADING THE PRESS

Wild and rich the oozings pour
From the press;
Leaner grows the tangled store
Of vintage, ever less:
Wine that kindles and entrances
Thus is made by one who dances.

SPRING

SANDRO BOTTICELLI

The Accademia of Florence

VENUS is sad among the wanton powers,
That make delicious tempest in the hours
Of April or are reckless with their flowers :
      Through umbrageous orange-trees
      Sweeps, mid azure swirl, the Breeze,
      That with clipping arms would seize
      Eôs, wind-inspired and mad,
      In wind-tightened muslin clad,
      With one tress for stormy wreath
      And a bine between her teeth.
      Flora foots it near in frilled,
      Vagrant skirt, with roses filled ;
      Pinks and gentians spot her robe
      And the curled acanthus-lobe

22

SPRING

Edges intricate her sleeve ;
Rosy briars a girdle weave,
Blooms are brooches in her hair :
Though a vision debonair,
Thriftless, venturesome, a grace
Disingenuous lights her face ;
Curst she is, uncertain-lipped,
Riggishly her dress is whipped
By little gusts fantastic.   Will she deign
To toss her double-roses, or refrain ?

These riot by the left side of the queen ;
Before her face another group is seen :
In ordered and harmonic nobleness,
Three maidens circle o'er the turf—each dress
Blown round the tiptoe shape in lovely folds
Of air-invaded white ; one comrade holds
Her fellow's hand on high, the foremost links
Their other hands in chain that lifts and sinks.

SPRING

Their auburn tresses ripple, coil or sweep;
Gems, amulets and fine ball-fringes keep
Their raiment from austereness.　With reserve
The dancers in a garland slowly curve.
They are the Graces in their virgin youth;
And does it touch their Deity with ruth
That they must fade when Eros speeds his dart?
Is this the grief and forethought of her heart?

For she is sad, although fresh myrtles near
Her figure chequer with their leaves the drear,
Grey chinks that through the orange-trees appear :

    Clothed in spring-time's white and red,
    She is tender with some dread,
    As she turns a musing head
    Sideways mid her veil demure;
    Her wide eyes have no allure,
    Dark and heavy with their pain.
    She would bless, and yet in vain

SPRING

Is her troubled blessing : Love,
Blind and tyrannous above,
Shoots his childish flame to mar
Those without defect, who are
Yet unspent and cold with peace ;
While, her sorrow to increase,
Hermes, leader of her troop—
His short cutlass on the loop
Of a crimson cloak, his eye
Clear in its fatality—
Rather seems the guide of ghosts
To the dead, Plutonian coasts,
Than herald of Spring's immature, gay band :
He plucks a ripened orange with his hand.

The tumult and the mystery of earth,
When woods are bleak and flowers have sudden birth,
When love is cruel, follow to their end
The God that teaches Shadows to descend,

SPRING

But pauses now awhile, with solemn lip
And left hand laid victorious on his hip.
The triumph of the year without avail
Is blown to Hades by blue Zephyr's gale.
Across the seedling herbage coltsfoot grows
Between the tulip, heartsease, strawberry-rose,
Fringed pinks and dull grape-hyacinth.   Alas,
At play together, through the speckled grass
Trip Youth and April: Venus, looking on,
Beholds the mead with all the dancers gone.

A PORTRAIT

BARTOLOMMEO VENETO

The Städel'sche Institut at Frankfurt

A CRYSTAL, flawless beauty on the brows
Where neither love nor time has conquered space
On which to live ; her leftward smile endows
The gazer with no tidings from the face ;
About the clear mounds of the lip it winds with silvery pace
    And in the umber eyes it is a light
Chill as a glowworm's when the moon embrowns an August night.

She saw her beauty often in the glass,
Sharp on the dazzling surface, and she knew
The haughty custom of her grace must pass :
Though more persistent in all charm it grew

27

A PORTRAIT

As with a desperate joy her hair across her throat she drew
    In crinkled locks stiff as dead, yellow snakes . . .
Until at last within her soul the resolution wakes

    She will be painted, she who is so strong
    In loveliness, so fugitive in years :
    Forth to the field she goes and questions long
    Which flowers to choose of those the summer bears ;
She plucks a violet larkspur,—then a columbine appears
    Of perfect yellow,—daisies choicely wide ;
These simple things with finest touch she gathers in her pride.

    Next on her head, veiled with well-bleachen white
    And bound across the brow with azure-blue,
    She sets the box-tree leaf and coils it tight
    In spiky wreath of green, immortal hue ;
Then, to the prompting of her strange, emphatic insight true,
    She bares one breast, half-freeing it of robe,
And hangs green-water gem and cord beside the naked globe.

A PORTRAIT

So was she painted and for centuries
    Has held the fading field-flowers in her hand
    Austerely as a sign.   O fearful eyes
    And soft lips of the courtesan who planned
ɔ give her fragile shapeliness to art, whose reason spanned
        Her doom, who bade her beauty in its cold
ɩd vacant eminence persist for all men to behold !

    She had no memories save of herself
    And her slow-fostered graces, naught to say
    Of love in gift or boon ; her cruel pelf
    Had left her with no hopes that grow and stay ;
e found default in everything that happened night or day,
        Yet stooped in calm to passion's dizziest strife
ɩd gave to art a fair, blank form, unverified by life.

    Thus has she conquered death : her eyes are fresh,
    Clear as her frontlet jewel, firm in shade
    And definite as on the linen mesh

A PORTRAIT

Of her white hood the box-tree's sombre braid,
That glitters leaf by leaf and with the year's waste will not fade
The small, close mouth, leaving no room for breath,
In perfect, still pollution smiles—Lo, she has conquered death

SAINT KATHARINE OF ALEXANDRIA

BARTOLOMMEO VENETO

The Städel'sche Institut at Frankfurt

A LITTLE wreath of bay about her head,
The Virgin-Martyr stands, touching her wheel
With finger-tips that from the spikes of steel
Shrink, though a thousand years she has been dead.
She bleeds each day as on the day she bled;
Her pure, gold cheeks are blanched, a cloudy seal
Is on her eyes; the mouth will never feel
Pity again; the yellow hairs are spread
Downward as damp with sweat; they touch the rim
Of the green bodice that to blackness throws
The thicket of bay-branches sharp and trim
Above her shoulder: open landscape glows
Soft and apart behind her to the right,
Where a swift shallop crosses the moonlight.

SAINT SEBASTIAN

CORREGGIO

The Dresden Gallery

BOUND by thy hands, but with respect unto thine eyes how fre
Fixed on Madonna, seeing all that they were born to see!
    The Child thine upward face hath sighted,
        Still and delighted;
Oh, bliss when with mute rites two souls are plighted!

As the young aspen-leaves rejoice, though to the stem held ti
In the soft visit of the air, the current of the light,
    Thou hast the peril of a captive's chances,
        Thy spirit dances,
Caught in the play of Heaven's divine advances.

hile cherubs straggle on the clouds of luminous, curled fire,
he Babe looks through them, far below, on thee with soft desire.
    Most clear of bond must they be reckoned—
        No joy is second
heirs whose eyes by other eyes are beckoned.

hough arrows rain on breast and throat they have no power to hurt,
hile thy tenacious face they fail an instant to avert.
    Oh might my eyes, so without measure,
        Feed on their treasure,
world with thong and dart might do its pleasure!

A 'SANT' IMAGINE'

FIORENZO DI LORENZO

The Städel'sche Institut at Frankfurt

A HOLY Picture—variably fair
In colour and fantastic in device!
    With what an ecstasy is laid
    The pattern of this red brocade,
Blood-red above Madonna's seat for glory;
  But gold and black behind the victor-two
      Who, full in view
  Of the great, central form, in thought
  Live through the martyrdom they wrought;
Afresh, with finer senses, suffer and despair.
     Why is their story
Set in such splendour one must note the nice
Edge of the arras and the glancing tone
Of jacinth floor, pale rose before the Virgin's throne?

34

A 'SANT' IMAGINE'

A young St. Christopher, with Umbria's blue
Clear in his eyes, stands nobly to the right
    And questions how the thing may hap
    The little, curious, curled-up chap,
That clings almost astride upon his shoulder
    And with uncertain baby-fingers lays
      A pat of praise
  On the crisp, propping head, should press
  Upon him to acute distress.
Vainly he turns ; within the child's eyes is no clue ;
      And he with colder
Heart must give succour to the sad in plight :
To him no secrets of his doom are known ;
Who suffers fate to load must bear the load alone.

And wherefore doth Madonna thus look down
So wistful toward the book upon her knees?
Has she no comfort ?   Is there need
Within the Scriptures she should read

A 'SANT' IMAGINE'

Who to the living Word her bosom presses ?
With bliss of her young Babe so near,
  Is it not drear
 Darkly from books to understand
 What bodes his coming to the land ?
Alas, as any other child he catches at her gown
  And, with caresses,
Breaks on her still *Magnificat* : to ease
And give air to her spirit with her own
Christ she must hold communion in great songs alone.

She bows and sheds no comfort on the boy
Whose face turns on her full of bleeding tears,
 Sebastian, with the arrows' thrill
 Intolerable to him still,
 Full of an agony that has no measure,
 That cannot rise, grow to the height and wane,
  Being simple pain

A 'SANT' IMAGINE'

That to his nature is as bound
As anguish to the viol's sound :
He suffers as the sensitive enjoy ;
            And, as their pleasure,
His pain is hid from common eyes and ears.
Wide-gaping as for air, breathing no moan,
His delicate, exhausted lips are open thrown.

And now back to the picture's self we come,
Its subtle, glowing spirit ; turn our eyes
        From those grave, isolated, strange
        Figures, to feel how sweet the range
    Of colour in the marbles, with what grace is
    Sebastian's porphyry-column reared aloft !
            How waving, soft
And fringed the palm-branch of the stave
Saint Christopher exalts !—they must have all things brave
About them who are born for martyrdom :

A 'SANT' IMAGINE'

The fine, stern faces
Refuse so steadily what they despise;
The world will never mix them with her own—
They choose the best, and with the best are left alone.

THE RESCUE

TINTORETTO

The Dresden Gallery

GREY tower, green sea, dark armour and clear curves

Of shining flesh; the tower built far into the sea

And the dark armour that of one coming to set her free

    Who, white against the chamfered base,

    From fetters that her noble limbs enlace

        Bows to confer

        Herself on her deliverer :

  He, dazzled by the splendid gift,

Steadies himself against his oar, ere he is strong to lift

        And strain her to his breast :

Her powerful arms lie in such heavy rest

Across his shoulder, though he swerves

39

And staggers with her weight, though the wave buoys,
Then slants the vessel, she maintains his form in poise.

Her sister-captive, seated on the side
Of the swayed gondola, her arched, broad back in strain,
Strikes her right ankle, eager to discumber it of chain,
    Intent upon her work, as though
    It were full liberty ungyved to go.
       She will not halt,
    But spring delighted to the salt,
When fetterless her ample form
Can beat the refluence of the waves back to their crested storm
    Has she indeed caught sight
Of that blithe tossing pinnace on the white
    Scum of the full, up-bearing tide?
The rose-frocked rower-boy, in absent fit
Or modesty, surveys his toe and smiles at it.

Her bondage irks not; *she* has very truth
Of freedom who within her lover's face can seek

THE RESCUE

For answer to her eyes, her breath, the blood within her cheek—

    A soul so resolute to bless

    She has forgot her shining nakedness

        And to her peer

    Presents immunity from fear :

As one half-overcome, half-braced,

The man's hand searches as he grips her undulating waist :

    So these pure twain espouse

And without ravishment, mistrust, or vows

    Of constancy fulfil their youth ;

In the rough niches of the wall behind

Their meeting heads, how close the trails of ivy wind !

VENUS AND MARS

SANDRO BOTTICELLI

The National Gallery

SHE is a fate, although
She lies upon the grass,
While satyrs shout *Ho, ho !*
At what she brings to pass ;
And nature is as free
Before her strange, young face
As if it knew that she
Were in her sovereign place,
With shading trees above.
The little powers of earth on woolly hips
Are gay as children round a nurse they love ;
Nor do they watch her lips.

42

VENUS AND MARS

A cushion, crimson-rose,
Beneath her elbow heaves ;
Her head, erect in pose
Against the laurel-leaves,
Is looped with citron hair
That cunning plaits adorn.
Beside her instep bare
And dress of crimpled lawn
Fine blades of herbage rise ;
The level field that circles her retreat
Is one grey-lighted green the early sky's
Fresh blue inclines to meet.

Her swathing robe is bound
With gold that is not new :
She rears from off the ground
As if her body grew
Triumphant as a stem
That hath received the rains,

43

VENUS AND MARS

Hath softly sunk with them,
And in an hour regains
Its height and settledness.
Yet are·her eyes alert; they search and weigh
The god, supine, who fell from her caress'
When love had had its sway.

He lies in perfect death
Of sleep that has no spasm;
It seems his very breath
Is lifted from a chasm,
So sunk he lies.   His hair
In russet heaps is spread;
Thus couches in its lair
A creature that is dead:
But, see, his nostrils scent
New joy and tighten palpitating nerves,
Although his naked limbs, their fury spent,
Are fallen in wearied curves.

44

VENUS AND MARS

Athwart his figure twist
Some wreathy folds of white,
Crossed by the languid wrist
And loose palm of his right,
Wan hand; the other drops
Its fingers down beside
The coat of mail that props
His shoulder; crimson-dyed,
His cloak winds under him;
One leg is stretched, one raised in arching lines:
Thus, opposite the queen, his body slim
And muscular reclines.

An impish satyr blows
The mottled conch in vain
Beside his ear that knows
No whine of the sea-strain;
Another tugs his spear,
One hides within his casque

VENUS AND MARS

Soft horns and jaunty leer ;
While one presumes to bask
Within his breastplate void
And rolls its tongue in open-hearted zest :
Above the sleeper, their dim wings annoyed,
The wasps have made a nest.

O tragic forms, the man,
The woman—he asleep,
She lone and sadder than
The dawn, too wise to weep
Illusion that to her
Is empire, to the earth
Necessity and stir
Of sweet, predestined mirth !
Ironical she sees,
Without regret, the work her kiss has done
And lives a cold enchantress doomed to please
Her victims one by one.

46

THE DEATH OF PROCRIS

PIERO DI COSIMO

The National Gallery

.AH, foolish Procris !—short and brown
She lies upon the leafy, littoral plain ;
Her scarlet cloak, her veil have both slipped down
       And rest
Across her loins ; the naked feet are bound
With sandals of dull gold, their thongs being wide
And interlaced ; the body's swelling side
Crushes the arm ; each sterile breast
Is grey ; upon the throat there is a stain
Of blood and on the hand along the ground.
       She gave no mortal cry,
But voiceless and consumed by drouth,

47

THE DEATH OF PROCRIS

Far from the town she might not gain,
> Beside a river-mouth
> She dragged herself to die.

Her auburn tresses part or coil
Below a wimple of most sombre blue;
They fleck the green of the luxuriant soil
> Or drift
Thinly athwart the outline of her ear.
Time has been passing since she last drew breath;
She has the humble, clay-cold look of death
Within the open world; no rift
Has come between the eyelids, of a hue
Monotonous—a paleness drear.

> Her brows attest no thought;
Her lips, that quick destruction stains,
Shall never kiss her husband, never sue
> For pardon: she remains
> A quarry none has sought.

48

THE DEATH OF PROCRIS

And thus she lies half-veiled, half-bare,
Deep in the midst of nature that abides
Inapprehensive she is lying there,
      So wan;
The flowers, the silver estuary afar—
These daisies, plantains, all the white and red
Field-blossoms through the leaves and grasses spread;
The water with its pelican,
Its flight of sails and its blue countrysides—
Unto themselves they are:
      The dogs sport on the sand,
The herons curve above the reeds
Or one by one descend the air,
      While lifelessly she bleeds
      From throat and dabbled hand.

Russet and large against the sky,
Two figures at her head and feet are seen;

THE DEATH OF PROCRIS

One is a solemn hound, one utterly

    A faun,

A creature of wild fashion, with black fell

On which a fleshy, furrèd ear loops out ;

Under his chin the boorish bristles sprout

Distinct ; an onyx-banded horn

Springs from each temple ; slender legs between

The herbage peep and well-

    Fleeced thighs ; his left hand grips

Her shoulder and the right along

Her forehead moves : his mellow eye

    Is indecisive ; strong,

    Coarse pity swells his lips.

The tall dog's vigil and the gaze

Of the wild man, by eagerness bent low,

Have each a like expression of amaze

    And deep,

Respectful yearning : these two watchers pass

THE DEATH OF PROCRIS

Out of themselves, though only to attain
Incomprehensible, half-wakened pain.
They cannot think nor weep
Above this perished jealousy and woe,
This prostrate, human mass ;
      But with vague souls they sit
And gaze, while tide and bloom and bird
Live on in their familiar ways,
      By mortal grief unstirred
      And never sad with it.

Yet autumn comes, there is the light
Born of October's lateness in the sky
And on the sea-side ; leaves have taken flight
      From yon,
Slim seedling-birch on the rivage, the flock
Of herons has the quiet of solitude,
That comes when chills on sunny air intrude ;
The little ships must soon be gone,

THE DEATH OF PROCRIS

And soon the pale and ruddy flowers shall die,
Save the untransient plants that block
      Their green out, ebon-clear,
Against the distance, while they drop,
On hound and satyr settled nigh,
      Red tassels that shall stop
      Till windy snows appear.

SAINT JEROME IN THE DESERT

COSIMO TURA

The National Gallery

SAINT JEROME kneels within the wilderness ;
Along the cavern's sandy channels press
The flowings of deep water.   On one knee,
       On one foot he rests his weight—
   A foot that rather seems to be
The clawed base of a pillar past all date
       Than prop of flesh and bone ;
   About his sallow, osseous frame
   A cinder-coloured cloak is thrown
   For ample emblem of his shame.

Grey are the hollowed rocks, grey is his head
And grey his beard that, formal and as dread

SAINT JEROME IN THE DESERT

As some Assyrian's on a monument,
    From the chin is sloping down.
  O'er his tonsure heaven has bent
A solid disc of unillumined brown;
    His scarlet hat is flung
  Low on the pebbles by a shoot
  Of tiny nightshade that among
  The pebbles has maintained a root.

He turns his face—yea, turns his body where
They front the cleanness of the sky and air;
We feel, although we see not, what he sees.
    From the hidden desert flows
  An uncontaminated breeze
That terrible in censure round him blows;
    While the horizons brim
  His eyes with silver glare and it
  Casts, in its purity, on him
  An accusation infinite.

SAINT JEROME IN THE DESERT

Sublime and fierce, he will not budge
Although each element becomes his judge:
For is not life the breath of God and thought
    God's own light across the brain?
  Yet he, in whom these powers have wrought,
Hath dared with slow and lusting flesh to stain
    Their operations clear
  As those of sunshine and the wind:
  He is unfit for sigh or tear,
  So whole the sin that he hath sinned,

Thus having done the man within him wrong.
He lifts his arm, the tendons of it strong
As rods, the fingers resolute and tense
    Round a flint-stone in the hand;
  Against his breast, with vehemence,
He aims a blow, as if at God's command.
    His breast of flint awaits
  Much flagellation; pleasure fills

SAINT JEROME IN THE DESERT

The body courage reinstates
Enduring what the spirit wills.

Dark wisdom, dread asceticism!—See,
The night-owl, set athwart a rock-bound tree
Below the cave, rolls pertinacious eyes
    On the penitence that bleeds,
  That in abashed absorption tries
To rouse the mere forgetfulness it needs.
    But lo! a white bird's wings
  Find on the cliff a resting-place :—
If man looks forth on unsoiled things,
  His own defilement he must face,

With somewhat of the hermit's rage of shame,
That only smarting chastisement can tame :
Yet Jerome's mood is humbler, surer far
    When, distressful penance done,

SAINT JEROME IN THE DESERT

His grey-bound volumes, his red Vulgate are
Laid on his lap and he within the sun
    Is writing, undismayed
  As the quiet cowherd who attends
  His kine, beneath a colonnade,
  Where yonder, ancient hill ascends.

METTUS CURTIUS

UNKNOWN

The National Gallery

He comes from yonder castle on the steep,
No Roman, but a lovely Christian knight,
With azure vest and florid mantle bright,
Blown, golden hair and youthful face flushed deep
For glory in the triumph of the leap.
Though his mild, amber horse rears back at sight
Of the red flames, though poised for thrust his right
Hand grasps a knife, his countenance doth keep
Soft as Saint Michael's with the devil at bay.
So sweet it is to cast one's life away
In the fresh pride and perfume of its breath!
He smiles to think how soon the cleft will close:
And see, a sun-brimmed cloud above him throws
Its white effulgence, as he fares to death.

A FÊTE CHAMPÊTRE

ANTOINE WATTEAU

The Dresden Gallery

A LOVELY, animated group
That picnic on a marble seat,
Where flaky boughs of beeches droop,
Where gowns in woodland sunlight glance,
Where shines each coy, lit countenance ;
While sweetness rules the air, most sweet
      Because the day
Is deep within the year that shall decay :

They group themselves around their queen,
This lady in the yellow dress,

A FÊTE CHAMPÊTRE

With bluest knots of ribbon seen
Upon her breast and yellow hair;
But the reared face proclaims *Beware !*
To him who twangs his viol less
      To speak his joy
Than her soon-flattered choiceness to annoy.

Beside her knee a damsel sits,
In petticoat across whose stripes
Of delicate decision flits
The wind that shows them blue and white
And primrose round a bodice tight—
As grey as is the peach that ripes :
      Her hair was spun
For Zephyrus among the threads to run.

She on love's varying theme is launched—
Ah, youth !—behind her, roses lie,
The latest, artless roses, blanched

A FÊTE CHAMPÊTRE

Around a hectic centre.   Two
Protesting lovers near her sue
And quarrel, Cupid knows not why :
      Withdrawn and tart,
One gallant stands in reverie apart.

Proud of his silk and velvet, each
Plum-tinted, of his pose that spurns
The company, his eyes impeach
A Venus on an ivied bank,
Who rests her rigorous, chill flank
Against a water-jet and turns
      Her face from those
Who wanton in the coloured autumn's close.

Ironical he views her shape of stone
And the harsh ivy and grey mound ;
Then sneers to think she treats her own

A FÊTE CHAMPÊTRE

Enchanted couples with contempt,
As though her bosom were exempt
From any care, while tints profound
      Touch the full trees
And there are warning notes in every breeze.

The coldness of mere pleasure when
Its hours are over cuts his heart:
That Love should rule the earth and men
For but a season year by year
And then must straightway disappear,
Even as the summer weeks depart,
      Has thrilled his brain
With icy anger and censorious pain.

Alas, the arbour-foliage now,
As cornfields when they lately stood
Awaiting harvest, bough on bough

A FÊTE CHAMPÊTRE

Is saffron.   Yonder to the left
A straggling rose-bush is bereft
Of the last roses of the wood ;
   For one or two
Still flicker where the balmy dozens grew.

On the autumnal grass the pairs
Of lovers couch themselves and raise
A facile merriment that dares
Surprise the vagueness of the sun
October to a veil has spun
About the heads and forest-ways—
   Delicious light
Of gold so pure it half-refines to white.

Yet Venus from this world of love,
Of haze and warmth has turned : as yet
None feels it save the trees above,

A FÊTE CHAMPÊTRE

The roses in their soft decline

And one ill-humoured libertine.

Soon shall all hearts forget

      The vows they swore

And the leaves strew the glade's untrodden floor.

A SHEPHERD-BOY

GIORGIONE

Hampton Court

A RADIANT, oval face: the hair
About the cheeks so blond in hue
It shades to greenness here and there
Against the ground of densest blue
A cloak flax-grey, a shirt of white,
That yellow spots of sunshine fleck;
The face aglow with southern light,
Deep, golden sunbrown on the neck;
Warm eyes, sweet mouth of the softest lips:
  Yea, though he is not playing,
  His hand a flute Pandean grips,
    Across one hole a finger laying.

A SHEPHERD-BOY

His flesh a golden haze, the line
Of cheek and chin is only made
By modulation, perfect, fine,
Of their rich colour into shade.
His curls have sometime veiled the top
Of the wide forehead,—we can see
How where the sunbeams might not stop
A subtle whiteness stretches, free
From the swarthy burning of their love :
    The opened shirt exposes
Fair skin that meets the stain above
    Half-coyly with its white and roses.

Not merely does he bear the sun
Thus visible on limb and head,
His countenance reveals him one
Of those whose characters are fed
By light—the largeness of its ways,
The breadth and patience in its joy.

A SHEPHERD-BOY

Evenings of sober azure, days
Of heat have influenced the lone boy
To dream with never a haunting thought,
    To be too calm for gladness
And in the hill-groves to have caught
    Hints of intensest summer sadness.

Yet pain can never overcast
A soul thus solemnly subdued
To muse upon an open past
Of sunshine, love and solitude.
Maternal nature and his own
Secluded mother are the sole
Companions he has ever known ;
His earliest innocence is whole :
His mouth, attuned to the silvan breeze,
    Is mobile with the blowing
Of notes beneath the olive-trees
    Or where an upland source is flowing.

67

A SHEPHERD-BOY

Ah, Golden Age, time has run back
And fetched you for our eyes to greet
And set you to repair our lack
Of splendour that is truly sweet,
By showing us how life can rear
Its children to enjoying sense
Of all that visits eye and ear,
Through days of restful reticence.
Delight will never be slow to come
     To youth that lays its finger
On the flute's stop and yet is dumb
     And loves with its dumb self to linger.

SAINT SEBASTIAN

ANTONELLO DA MESSINA

The Dresden Gallery

YOUNG Sebastian stands beside a lofty tree,
Rigid by the rigid trunk that branchlessly
 Lifts its column on the blue
 Of a heaven that takes
 Hyacinthine hue
 From a storm that wellnigh breaks.

Shadiness and thunder dout the zenith's light,
Yet a wide horizon still extends as bright
 As the lapis-lazuli;
 Poignant sunshine streams
 Over land and sky,
 With tempestuous, sunken beams.

SAINT SEBASTIAN

He who was a soldier late is standing now
Stript and fastened to the tree that has no bough,
 In the centre of a court,
 That is bound by walls
  Fancifully wrought,
 Over which the daylight falls.

Arch and chimney rise aloft into the air :
On the balconies are hung forth carpets rare
 Of an Eastern, vivid red ;
 Idle women lean
  Where the rugs are spread,
 Each with an indifferent mien.

On the marble of the courtyard, fast asleep,
Lies a brutish churl, his body in a heap ;
 Two hard-hearted comrades prate
 Where a portal shows

SAINT SEBASTIAN

Distance blue and great,
Stretching onward in repose.

And between the shafts of sandy-coloured tone
Slips a mother with her child : but all alone
Stays Sebastian in his grief.
What soul pities him !
Who shall bring relief
From the darts that pierce each limb ?

Naked, almost firm as sculpture, is his form,
Nobly set below the burthen of the storm ;
Shadow, circling chin and cheek,
Their ellipse defines,
Then the shade grows weak
And his face with noonday shines—

Shines as olive marble that reflects the mere
Radiance it receives upon a surface clear ;

SAINT SEBASTIAN

For we see no blessedness
On his visage pale,
　　Turned in its distress
Toward the heaven, without avail.

Massive is his mouth ; the upper lip is set
In a pained, protesting curve : his eyes have met
　　God within the darkening sky
　　And dispute His will,
　　　Dark, remorselessly
　　Fervent to dispute it still.

The whole brow is hidden by the chestnut hair,
That behind the back flows down in locks and there
　　Changes to a deeper grain.
　　Though his feet were strong,
　　　They are swoln with strain,
　　For he has been standing long.

72

SAINT SEBASTIAN

Captive, stricken through by darts, yet armed with power
That resents the coming on of its last hour,
    Sound in muscle is the boy,
    Whom his manhood fills
      With an acrid joy,
    Whom its violent pressure thrills.

But this force implanted in him must be lost
And its natural validity be crossed
    By a chill, disabling fate;
    He must stand at peace
      While his hopes abate,
    While his youth and vigour cease.

At his feet a mighty pillar lies reversed;
So the virtue of his sex is shattered, cursed:
    Here is martyrdom and not

SAINT SEBASTIAN

In the arrows' sting ;
This the bitter lot
His soul is questioning.

He, with body fresh for use, for pleasure fit,
With its energies and needs together knit
In an able exigence,
Must endure the strife,
Final and intense,
Of necessity with life.

Yet throughout this bold rebellion of the saint
Noonday's brilliant air has carried no complaint.
Lo, across the solitude
Of the storm two white,
Little clouds obtrude
Storm-accentuating light !

THE MAGDALEN

TIMOTEO VITI

The Accademia at Bologna

THIS tender sylph of a maid
Is the Magdalen—this figure lone :
    Her attitude is swayed
    By the very breath she breathes,
The prayer of her being that takes no voice.
    Boulders, the grass enwreathes,
    Arch over her as a cave
    That of old an earthquake clave
    And filled with stagnant gloom :
Yet a woman has strength to choose it for her room.

    Her long, fair hair is allowed
To wander in its thick simpleness ;

THE MAGDALEN

The graceful tresses crowd
Unequal, yet close enough·
To have woven about her neck and breast
A wimple of golden stuff.
Though the rock behind is rude,
The sweetness of solitude
Is on her face, the soft
Withdrawal that in wild-flowers we have loved so oft.

Her mantle is scarlet-red
In folds of severe resplendency;
Her hair beneath is spread
Full-length; from its lower flakes
Her feet come forth in their naked charm:
A wind discreetly shakes
The scarlet raiment, the hair.
Her small hands, a tranquil pair,
Are laid together; her book
And cup of ointment furnish scantily her nook.

76

THE MAGDALEN

She is happy the livelong day,
Yet her thoughts are often with the past;
    Her sins are done away,
    They can give her no annoy.
She is white—oh ! infinitely clean
    And her heart throbs with joy ;
    Besides, there is joy in heaven
    That her sins are thus forgiven ;
    And she thinks till even-fall
Of the grace, the strangeness, the wonder of it all.

    She is shut from fellowship ;
How she loved to mingle with her friends !
    To give them eyes and lip ;
    She lived for their sake alone ;
Not a braid of her hair, not a rose
    Of her cheek was her own :
    And she loved to minister

77

THE MAGDALEN

To any in want of her,
All service was so sweet :
Now she must stand all day on lithe, unsummoned feet.

Among the untrodden weeds
And moss she is glad to be remote ;
She knows that when God needs
From the sinning world relief,
He will find her thus with the wild bees,
The doves and the plantain-leaf,
Waiting in a perfect peace
For His kingdom's sure increase,
Waiting with a deeper glow
Of patience every day, because He tarrieth so.

By her side the box of nard
Unbroken . . . God is a great way off ;
She loves Him : it is hard
That she may not now even spread

THE MAGDALEN

The burial-spice, who would gladly keep

  The tomb where He lay dead,

  As it were her rocky cave;

  And fold the linen and lave

  The napkin that once bound

His head; no place for her pure arts is longer found.

  And these are the things that hurt;

For the rest she gives herself no pain:

  She wears no camel shirt,

  She uses nor scourge, nor rod;

But bathes her fair body in the well

  And keeps it pure for God:

  The beauty, that He hath made

  So bright, she guards in the shade,

  For, as an angel's dress,

Spotless she must preserve her new-born loveliness.

  Day by day and week by week,

She lives and muses and makes no sound;

THE MAGDALEN

She has no words to speak

The joy that her desert brings :

In her heart there is a song

And yet no song she sings.

Since the word *Rabboni* came

Straightway at the call of her name

And the Master reproved,

It seems she has no choice—her lips have never moved.

She stole away when the pale

Light was trembling on the garden-ground

And others told the tale,

Christ was risen ; she roamed the wide,

Fearful countries of the wilderness

And many a river-side,

Till she found her destined grot,

South, in France, a woody spot,

Where she is often glad,

Musing on those great days when she at first grew sad.

A PEN-DRAWING OF LEDA

SODOMA

The Grand Duke's Palace at Weimar

Leda lovely, wild and free,

rawing her gracious Swan down through the grass to see

ertain round eggs without a speck :

nd plunged in the reeds and one dinting the downy neck,

lthough his hectoring bill

apes toward her tresses,

ws the fondled creature to her will.

joys to bend in the live light

stening body toward her love, how much more bright !

hough on her breast the sunshine lies

reads its affluence on the wide curves of her waist and thighs,

o her meek, smitten gaze

There her hand presses

wan's white neck sink Heaven's concentred rays.

F

MARRIAGE OF BACCHUS AND ARIADNE

TINTORETTO

The Ducal Palace at Venice

DARK sea-water round a shape
Hung about the loins with grape,
Hair the vine itself, in braids
On the brow—thus Bacchus wades
Through the water to the shore.
Strange to deck with hill-side store
Limbs that push against the tide ;
Strange to gird a wave-washed side
Foam should spring at and entwine—
Strange to burthen it with vine.

He has left the trellised isle,
Left the harvest vat awhile,
Left the Maenads of his troop,
Left his Fauns' midsummer group

And his leopards far behind,
By lone Dia's coast to find
Her whom Theseus dared to mock.
Queenly on the samphire rock
Ariadne sits, one hand
Stretching forth at Love's command.

Love is poised above the twain,
Zealous to assuage the pain
In that stately woman's breast;
Love has set a starry crest
On the once dishonoured head;
Love entreats the hand to wed,
Gently loosening out the cold
Fingers toward that hoop of gold
Bacchus, tremblingly content
To be patient, doth present.

In his eyes there is the pain
Shy, dumb passions can attain

MARRIAGE OF BACCHUS AND ARIADNE

In the valley, on the skirt
Of lone mountains, pine-begirt;
Yearning pleasure such as pleads
In dark wine that no one heeds
Till the feast is ranged and lit.
But his mouth—what gifts in it!
Though the round lips do not dare
Aught to proffer, save a prayer.

Is he not a mendicant
Who has almost died of want?
Through far countries he has roved,
Blessing, blessing, unbeloved;
Therefore is he come in weed
Of a mortal bowed by need,
With the bunches of the grape
As sole glory round his shape:
For there is no god that can
Taste of pleasure save as man.

THE FIGURE OF VENUS IN 'SPRING'

SANDRO BOTTICELLI

The Accademia of Florence

I.

A SIMPLE lady full of heavy thought :
Behind her neck the myrtle-bowers lie cold ;
Her robe is white, her carmine mantle rolled
And lifted on her arm that beareth nought :
A flame-tipped arrow in its arc is brought
Above by Eros ; ornaments of gold
Are crossed chainwise about her chest to hold
The unfilled breasts ; her right hand as she sought
To bless is lifted and then stays at pause
As fearful to cast sorrow for delight
On her girl-votaries.   Must her coming cause
Their stately freedom quite to disappear ?
Brings Love in truth a bitterness to blight
The yet unstricken gladness of the year ?

FIGURE OF VENUS IN 'SPRING'

II

Or is it Destiny that doth compel
Her hand to stay its blessing?   On her right
Three virgins, flowerless, slow of step, unite
In dance, as they were guided by the spell
Of some Choragus imperceptible :
Beside them Hermes lifts his wand to smite
An orange from the bough ; they keep in sight
The severing of the golden fruit for hell.
What boots it therefore that so light of breath
Comes Flora, from her lapful tossing flowers,
Come Zephyrus and fleeing nymph, if these
Are travelling wanton toward the infernal powers ;
If the stern Moirai move beneath the trees
With eyes fixed on the harbinger of death ?

APOLLO AND MARSYAS

PERUGINO

The Louvre

FAIR stands Apollo,
Magnanimous his figure sways :
    He deigns to follow
The brutish notes that Marsyas plays ;
And waits in haughty, vengeful peace,
    One hand on his hip,
While the fingers of the other quietly slip
      Round a staff.   He does not raise
      His eyes, nor move his lip.

    Breeze-haunted tresses,
Worn proudly, float around his head ;
    His brow confesses
No wrath—and yet a sky grows dead

APOLLO AND MARSYAS

And silent thus, when fatal bolts
        Treasure up their might
Underneath its secret and attentive light.
        Lifted by a cord of red
        His lyre hangs full in sight.

        His face supremely
Is set against the lucid air ;
        And, as is seemly,
Round Marsyas' straining skull the bare
Knolls of the vale are dominant.
        ˙ Waters spread their way
By yon bridge and towers, developing the gay
        Sunshine-blueness everywhere :
        The god is bright as they.

        Although his colour
Is of an ivory-olive and
        His locks are duller
Than his pale skin, that, scarcely tanned,

APOLLO AND MARSYAS

Flushes to carmine at the knee,—
      Gracious, heavenly wit
From his members such effulgence doth emit,
      Mortals must admiring stand
      Simply for awe of it.

      Unapprehending,
Absorbed, the brown, inferior man,
      On his tune spending
All honest power, believes he can
Put the young shepherd-god to shame.
      Scrutinise and hate
His spiritless brows, the red down on his pate,
      The diligent eyes that scan
      His fingers as they grate !

      The landscape spreadeth
In clarity for many a mile ;
      No light it sheddeth
Through stream and sky upon the vile,

APOLLO AND MARSYAS

Painstaking herdsman at his task.
    Summer brings no ease,
He misses the glow on the olive-green trees:
    A gyrfalcon stoops meanwhile
    A wild duck's head to seize.

    Wood-nightshade shooting
Purple blossom and yellow spark,
    Or scarlet fruiting,
By Marsyas' uncouth limbs we mark,
Where anxious and infirm he sits;
    The poet's feet are placed
On a soil rich-flowering violets have enlaced
    And the daphne-bush springs dark
    Behind his loins and waist.

    To end the matter,
He gives an ear to the abhorred
    Strains of the satyr,
Counting it worthy to afford

APOLLO AND MARSYAS

Grace to so confident a skill;

>   For he first did try

His strength and the rival did not fetch a sigh:

>   Lo, his rich-wrought heptachord

>   In silence he laid by.

>   Shame and displeasure—

The god of inspiration set

>   To hear a measure

Of halting pace ! But he will whet

A knife and without comment flay

>   The immodest faun,

Fearing poets should, indifferent through scorn,

>   License all that hinds beget

>   Or zealots feeble-born.

>   There is a sadness

Upon the lids, the mouth divine;

>   He loathes the badness

>   Of what disturbs his senses fine,

APOLLO AND MARSYAS

But calmly sorrows, not that doom
  Should harry ill-desert,
But that the offender callous, unalert
  To contempt or threatening sign,
  So grossly must be hurt.

THE BLOOD OF THE REDEEMER

GIOVANNI BELLINI

The National Gallery

Sunrise is close: the upper sky is blue
That has been darkness; and the day is new,
Bleaching yon little town: where the white hue,
　　Spread blank on the horizon, skirts
The night-mass there is strife and wavy rush
　　　　Of beams in flush.

But, as the amber-spotted clouds unroll,
One stands in shade of a dark aureole;
His deeply-folded loin-cloth and His whole
　　Wan body by the changing air
Made spectral, though the very wounds we see
　　　　Of Calvary.

93

THE BLOOD OF THE REDEEMER

Is He indeed the Christ? Those transverse beams
Of yon high cross confine Him not; it seems
Simply a token. Walking as in dreams
    He has paced onward and holds forth
Indifferent His pierced palm: O Life, O Clay,
        Our fears allay!

But to the people wert Thou crucified;
To eyes that see, behold, Thou dost abide
Dying for ever. Thus Thine Eastertide
    Breaks over Thee,—the crown of thorn
Laid by, but the whole breaking heart in quick
        Sorrow and sick.

The dawn is blue among the hills and white
Above their tops; a gladness creeps in sight
Across the silver-russet slopes, but night
    Obscures the mortal ebb and flow
Flushing Thy veins; Thy lips in strife for breath
        Are full of death.

THE BLOOD OF THE REDEEMER

For Thou art bleeding, bleeding; we can trace
Naught but a dizzy sickness in Thy face;
Thine eyes behold us not, yet round the place

    Whence flows Thy blood Thy conscious palm
With fervour of unbated will doth cling,

        Forcing its spring.

Thou standest not on earth, but raised apart
On a stone terrace, rich in cunning art;
Behind Thee, figures, diligent to start

    An altar-flame, in low relief
Are traced on tablets of a marble ledge

        At the floor's edge.

Blithe Pagan youths sculptured behind Thee go
Processional to sacrifice; some blow
A horn, some feed the censer, none can know

    What he should do; but Thou dost give
Thyself and consecrate their rites, how vain,

        O Lamb fresh slain!

THE BLOOD OF THE REDEEMER

Is it Thy Father's house, this pavement rare
Of chequered marbles, pale and brown, and there
For Thy belovèd thus must Thou prepare

    A place ?—Across the burnished floor,
Save that an uplift urn its stream hath stopped,
        Thy blood had dropped.

Once crucified and once given to the crowd,
But to Thy Church for aye a Victim vowed,
Thou dost not die, Thy head is never bowed

    In death: we must be born again;
Thus dying by our side from day to day
        Thou art the Way.

An angel kneels beside, in yellow sleeves
And robe of lovely, limpid blue; he heaves
With steady hand a chalice that receives

    The torrent of the precious blood.
His ruddy hair, crisp, rising from the roots,
        Falls in volutes.

THE BLOOD OF THE REDEEMER

Was he the angel bidden to infuse
Strength, when the Saviour yearned and could not choose
To drink the cup?—He has bright, scarlet shoes,
    Plumes lit by the jay's piercing blue,
Yet kneels distressful service to perform
        By this gaunt form.

One thing they have alike ; the curls that fleck
The angel's temples in profusion deck
His Master's, silken on the staring neck.
    Marred Son of Man, Thou once wert fair
As Israel's ruddy King who faintest thus :
        Thou drawest us.

There is no light athwart these eastern skies
For us, no joy it is that Thou dost rise—
Our hope, our strength is in Thy sacrifice :
    To-day, to-morrow must Thou die,
For ever drawing all men to Thy feet,
        O Love most sweet !

G   97

THE SLEEPING VENUS

GIORGIONE

The Dresden Gallery

HERE is Venus by our homes
And resting on the verdant swell
Of a soft country flanked with mountain domes :
She has left her archèd shell,
Has left the barren wave that foams,
Amid earth's fruitful tilths to dwell.

  Nobly lighted while she sleeps
  As sward-lands or the corn-field sweeps,
  Pure as are the things that man
  Needs for life and using can

THE SLEEPING VENUS

Never violate nor spot—
Thus she slumbers in no grot,
But on open ground,
With the great hill-sides around.

And her body has the curves,
The same extensive smoothness seen
In yonder breadths of pasture, in the swerves
Of the grassy mountain-green
That for her propping pillow serves :
There is a sympathy between
    Her and Earth of largest reach,
    For the sex that forms them each
    Is a bond, a holiness,
    That unconsciously must bless
    And unite them, as they lie
    Shameless underneath the sky
    A long, opal cloud
    Doth in noontide haze enshroud.

99

THE SLEEPING VENUS

O'er her head her right arm bends ;
And from the elbow raised aloft
Down to the crossing knees a line descends
Unimpeachable and soft
As the adjacent slope that ends
In chequered plain of hedge and croft.

    Circular as lovely knolls,
    Up to which a landscape rolls
    With desirous sway, each breast
    Rises from the level chest,
    One in contour, one in round—
    Either exquisite, low mound
    Firm in shape and given
    To the August warmth of heaven.

With bold freedom of incline,
With an uttermost repose,
From hip to herbage-cushioned foot the line
Of her left leg stretching shows

THE SLEEPING VENUS

Against the turf direct and fine,
Dissimilar in grace to those
    Little bays that in and out
    By the ankle wind about;
    Or that shallow bend, the right
    Curled-up knee has brought to sight
    Underneath its bossy rise,
    Where the loveliest shadow lies !
    Charmèd umbrage rests
    On her neck and by her breasts.

Her left arm remains beside
The plastic body's lower heaves,
Controlled by them, as when a river-side
With its sandy margin weaves
Deflections in a lenient tide ;
Her hand the thigh's tense surface leaves,
    Falling inward.   Not even sleep
    Dare invalidate the deep,

THE SLEEPING VENUS

Universal pleasure sex
Must unto itself annex —
Even the stillest sleep; at peace,
More profound with rest's increase,
She enjoys the good
Of delicious womanhood.

Cheek and eyebrow touch the fold
Of the raised arm that frames her hair,
Her braided hair in colour like to old
Copper glinting here and there:
While through her skin of olive-gold
The scarce carnations mount and share
Faultlessly the oval space
Of her temperate, grave face.
Eyelids underneath the day
Wrinkle as full buds that stay,
Through the tranquil, summer hours,
Closed although they might be flowers;

THE SLEEPING VENUS

The red lips shut in
Gracious secrets that begin.

On white drapery she sleeps,
That fold by fold is stained with shade ;
Her mantle's ruddy pomegranate in heaps
For a cushion she has laid
Beneath her; and the glow that steeps
Its grain of richer depth is made
By an overswelling bank,
Tufted with dun grasses rank.
From this hillock's outer heaves
One small bush defines its leaves
Broadly on the sober blue
The pale cloud-bank rises to,
Whilst it sinks in bland
Sunshine on the distant land.

Near her resting-place are spread,
In deep or greener-lighted brown,

THE SLEEPING VENUS

Wolds, that half-withered by the heat o'erhead,
Press up to a little town
Of castle, archway, roof and shed,
Then slope in grave continuance down :

    On their border, in a group,
    Trees of brooding foliage droop
    Sidelong ; and a single tree
    Springs with bright simplicity,
    Central from the sunlit plain.
    Of a blue no flowers attain,
    On the fair, vague sky
    Adamantine summits lie.

And her resting is so strong
That while we gaze it seems as though
She had lain thus the solemn glebes among
In the ages far ago
And would continue, till the long,
Last evening of Earth's summer glow

THE SLEEPING VENUS

In communion with the sweet
Life that ripens at her feet:
We can never fear that she
From Italian fields will flee,
For she does not come from far,
She is of the things that are;
And she will not pass
While the sun strikes on the grass.

A PIETÀ

CARLO CRIVELLI

Lord Dudley's Collection

A MOTHER bent on the body of her Son,
    Fierce tears and wrinkles around her eyes,—
        She has open, stiffened lips
        And an almost lolling tongue,
        But her face is full of cries :
Almost it seems that the dead has done her wrong,
        Almost it seems in her strife
    Of passion she would shake the dead to life.
        His body has been sold
    For silver and crucified ; but He—
    She laughs—from death He can recover ;
    E'en now whatever He saith shall be :
She will win Him, He shall kiss and love her.

A PIETÀ

His body, once blond, is soiled now and opaque
 With the solemn ochres of the tomb;
   The thorns on his brow are green
   And their fine tips folded in
   (Through the forehead forcing room)
By a swathe of the delicate, lifted skin:
   The half-closed eyes show grey,
 Leaden fissures; the dead man's face is clay;
   And though the lips for breath
 Leave room, there is no breathing, nor are
 They gaping eagerly; but parted
 And vacant as a house-door left ajar,
From which the owner of the house has started.

A loin-cloth many-folded is on his thighs;
 One hand has fall'n crookt across the hood
   Of his mother, one is held
   With awe by the Magdalen,
   Who darkly has understood

A PIETÀ

From the prayer on the cross, Christ must die for men.
That He once made hearts to burn
By the way He is touched alone we learn ;
No beauty to desire
Is here—stiffened limb and angry vein
And a belt, 'neath the hirsute nipple,
Of flesh that, flaccid and dragged from the strain
Of the cross, swells the waist with sinuous ripple.

Yet there is such subtle intercourse between
The hues and the passion is so frank
One is soothed, one feels it good
To be of this little group
Of mourners close to the rank,
Deep wounds, as to tend their unclean dead they stoop.
How softly falls in a streak
Christ's blanched tress toward his Mother's tear-burnt cheek
And how her sleeve of peach

A PIETA

That crosses the corpse's grimy gold
Gives it lustre! Her dark-hued kirtle
Is of the green that clouded sea-pools hold;
Her hood takes light like smooth leaves of the myrtle.

'Neath the third halo, wrought on a burnished ground
Of leafy stamp, is John's wailing face:
He shrieks; but he does not lift
The body into the grave:
Beside him in noble grace
Bows the Magdalen, who, putting forth a brave
Hand, 'twixt her finger and thumb
Lifts the Redeemer's arm and with a dumb
Wonder looks in the hole
Scooped by the large, round nail: *So they hurt
What one loves!* Yet about this silent creature's
Suppression there is promise; an alert
And moving faith prompts the vigilant features.

A PIETÀ

O glorious spring of the brow, simple arch
    Of the head that once was sunk so low
        With the outpoured box of nard!
        O solemn, dun-crimson mass
        Of hair, on the indigo
Of the bodice that in curling wave doth pass!
        How exquisite, set between
    This blue and a vest of translucent green,
        The glimpse of scarlet belt;
    Or the glow, the almost emerald line,
    Round the neck where the hood bends over
    Such faint reds of the mantle as incline
To the sorrel-seed or the ripened clover!

So it comes to pass that to this reticent
    And tender woman there is given sight
        Of Christ new-born from the tomb:
        The mother sees not her Son
        In whom her soul doth delight,

A PIETÀ

She knows Him not, nor the work his cross hath done:

>   But to Mary with the sealed

> Lips and hard patience Jesus is revealed.

>   His mother clasps his form,

> Craving for miracle and must lack

> For ever response to her passion:

> The dead, if indeed we would win them back,

Must be won in their own love's larger fashion.

THE VIRGIN, CHILD AND ST. JOHN

LORENZO DI CREDI

Lord Dudley's Collection

A SPREADING strawberry-tree
Embowers an altar-throne;
Behind its leaves we see
Fair waters blue in tone;
Sharp rocks confront the stream and soft
Summits and misty towers:
But sweet Madonna in a croft
Is resting, brimmed with flowers.

Anemones are here;
How sturdily they grow,

112

THE VIRGIN, CHILD AND ST. JOHN

Their brown-stemmed heads in clear
    Design against the flow
Of the thin current scarce astir !
    Through scrambling cresses strike
Petals of varied lavender
    In chalice and in spike.

    The summer light in streams
    Has fallen where it can stray
    On the blond girl who dreams
    So lazily all day.
Dropt eyelids of a differing curve,
    Deep-dinted lips austere,
Some curious grace of visage serve,
    Half-wayward, half-severe.

    No stain her cheek has got ;
    Its sun-blanch is complete,
    Save where one little spot
    Sweats, rosy with the heat.

THE VIRGIN, CHILD AND ST. JOHN

To keep that tender carmine free
    In lustre, the arbute
Shields with a multiplicity
    Of leaves its crimson fruit.

    Of corn-flower blue, with gold
    Her simple dress is sewn,
    A cloak's cerulean fold
    About her feet is thrown.
The lining of rich orange hue
    Is visible just where
The brilliant and the paler blue
    Would cruelly compare.

    Mid windings of her wrap,
    Her naked child upon
    The cradle of her lap
    Blesses adoring John,

114

THE VIRGIN, CHILD AND ST. JOHN

Whose flimsy, little shirt is tied
    With lilac scarf; the slim,
Gemmed crosier, propped against his side,
    Is far too long for him.

    Her scarlet-sandalled foot
    Soft resting-place has found;
    Cup-moss and daisy-root
    Are thick upon the ground
Almost as in our English dells :
    But here is columbine
And one of its pellucid bells
    Doth to the stream incline.

    How sweet to bless and pray
    And nothing understand,
    Warm in the lovely grey
    Of that illumined land.

THE VIRGIN, CHILD AND ST. JOHN

O boughs that such red berries bear,
　　O river-side of flowers,
No wonder Mary nurses there
　　Her Babe through summer hours !

L'EMBARQUEMENT POUR CYTHÈRE

ANTOINE WATTEAU

The Louvre

WHY starts this company so fair arrayed
   In pomegranate brocade,
Blue shoulder-cloak and barley-coloured dress
   Of flaunting shepherdess,
From shelter of the full-leaved, summer trees?
      What vague unease
Draws them in couples to a burnished boat?
   And wherefore from its prow,
Borne upward on a spiral, amber swirl
Of incense-light, themselves half-rose, half-pearl,
      So languorously doth float
   This flock of Loves that in degree
Fling their own hues as raiment on the sea;

L'EMBARQUEMENT POUR CYTHÈRE

While one from brandished censer

Flings wide a flame and smoke

Diffusive to provoke

The heavens to consummation and to spread

Refluence intenser

Of sun and cool

And tempting azure on that bed

Of splendour, that delicious, variant pool?

I see it now!

'Tis Venus' rose-veiled barque

And that great company ere dark

Must to Cythera, so the Loves prevail,

Adventurously sail.

O happy youth, that thus by Venus' guile

Is summoned to her fabulous,

Her crystal-burnished isle!

Her virile votaries are not slack

In ceremonious worship: bravely clad

L'EMBARQUEMENT POUR CYTHÈRE

In coats of flickering velvet, crimson-greys

Of corn-field gold, they leap to give her praise,

They grasp long staves, they joy as they were mad,

Drawing their dainty Beauties by the waist

    To that warm water-track.

What terror holds these noble damsels back ?

    Alack, what strange distaste

    Works in their hearts that thus

They sigh estranged ?   What pressure of what ill

    Turns their vague sweetness chill ?

      Why should they in debate,

    Beneath the nodding, summer trees,

    Dissentient dally and defer their fate ?

      Methinks none sees

    The statue of a Venus set

  Mid some fair trellis, in a lovely fret

    Of rose; her marble mien,

Secret, imperial, blank, no joy discovers

    In these uncertain lovers

L'EMBARQUEMENT POUR CYTHÈRE

That parley and grow pale:
Not one of them but is afraid to sail,
Save this firm-tripping dame who chooses
The voyage as a queen,
Conscious of what she wins and what she loses.
Her petticoat of fine-creased white
And, oh, her barley-coloured gown,
What miracles of silver-brown
They work amid the blues and puces!
As, full of whimsical delight
To mark a sister's half-abashed surrender,
Full proudly she doth bend her
Arched, amorous eyelids to commend her,
Gripping more tight
Her slender stave, that she may seem
Prompt to descend toward that dead, heated stream.

Her lover's face we lack,
Bent from us; yet we feel

L'EMBARQUEMENT POUR CYTHÈRE

How fervid his appeal,
s raised on tip-toe he his lofty dame addresses.
  Fine streaks of light across his raiment steal;
    For, though his cap is black,
When blossoms of japonica are spread
    In sunshine, whiter-smiling red
Was never seen than glistens on his sleeve.
    And how his furs flash to relieve
His lady's train of chrome!
Ah me, how long must these fond gallants blind
    The fears and waive the light distresses
      Of the coy girls who stay behind,
        Nor yet consent to roam
oward that soft, vermeil country far, so very far from home!

      First of the twain is seen
ale-tressed dame, couched on the grass, her bodice lambent green,
  Her frilling skirt of salmon and primrose

L'EMBARQUEMENT POUR CYTHÈRE

And green of many a flower before it blows
Who, pettish in remorse,
Awhile her lover's urgent hand refuses,
Then rises buoyant on its welcome force.
But, see, this third
Sweet lady is not stirred,
Though at her side a man
Half-kneels. Why is he pleading in her ear,
With eyes so near
That Paradise of light,
Where angles of the yellow, open fan
And gown the sunken pink
Of dying roses rim her bosom's white?
Her eyelids are full-drooped, but under
The lids is wonder;
And, at her skirt,
Ah, woe! in pilgrim hood and shirt
Dressed whimsical, a cunning Cupid-lad:
Soon shall the naked urchin be

L'EMBARQUEMENT POUR CYTHÈRE

Plunged in the depths of that cerulean sea
Where life runs warm, delicious, limpid, free.

So pause the nearer groups: to the land's rim
        Presses a dim
Confluence of hopes and angry amities:
'Forth to the fairy water, come; thine hand . . .
Nay then, by force; it is a god's command
And I by rape will bring thee to thy bliss.
What, sweet, so slow!'—'But ere I leave the land
Give me more vows; oh, bind thee to me fast;
        Speak, speak! I do not crave thy kiss.
To-morrow. . .'—'Love, the tide is rising swift;
Shall we not talk aboard? Your skirts are wet;
        If once I lift
You in!'—'Nay, nay, I cannot so forget
        The statue in the shade,
    The fountain-trickle by the leafy grot.

123

L'EMBARQUEMENT POUR CYTHÈRE

Might not this mad embarking be delayed
An instant ? '—' Dearest, would you cast your lot
       In that dull countryside,
             Where men abide
          Who must be buried ?   Note the swell
Of colour 'gainst the coast.'—' Then as you please.
How strange a story we shall have to tell ! '

             Two rowers wait ; one shoves
             The boat from shore, her cry
       From luscious mouth, her bosom lifted high
             Incite ; and one doth wait,
          With lip that hath full time to laugh
             And hand on oar,
       Conclusion of the soft debate.
Sudden the foremost of the fulgent Loves
             Seizes a staff
From wanton hand ; a thousand flambeaux pour

L'EMBARQUEMENT POUR CYTHÈRE

Their plumy smoke upon the kindled breeze
That wafts these silken loiterers to submerging seas.

Now are they gone: a change is in the light,
The iridescent ranges wane,
The waters spread: ere fall of night
The red-prowed shallop will have passed from sight
And the stone Venus by herself remain
Ironical above that wide, embrowning plain.

NOTE

By the kind permission of the Editor, *L'Indifférent*, *La Gioconda*, *The Faun's Punishment*, and *Saint Sebastian* (Correggio), are reprinted from *The Academy*.

Underneath the Bough

Underneath the Bough
A Book of Verses by
Michael Field

London   George Bell and Sons   York Street
Covent Garden and New York   Mdcccxciij

" A Book of Verses underneath the Bough,
A Jug of Wine, a Loaf of Bread, and thou
Beside me singing in the Wilderness.
Oh, Wilderness were Paradise enow !"

INVOCATION

THEE, *Apollo, in a ring*
    We encompass, carolling
Of the flowers, fruits and creatures
    That thy features
Do express, and by thy side
Live their life half-deified :
Grasshoppers that round thee spring
From their mirth no minute sparing ;
Hawk and griffin arrow-eyed ;
Cock the gracious day declaring ;
Olive that can only flourish
Where the fruiting sunbeams nourish ;
Laurel that can never fade,
That in winter doth incline her
Lustrous branches to embraid
Chaplets for the lyric brow ;
The white swan, that fair diviner,
Who in death a bliss descrying
Sings her sweetest notes a-dying :
These, all these, to thee we vow,
We thy nymphs who in a ring
Dance around thee, carolling.

THE FIRST BOOK OF SONGS

THE TABLE OF THE FIRST BOOK

THE FIRST BOOK OF SONGS

MORTAL, if thou art beloved,
  Life's offences are removed :
All the fateful things that checkt thee,
Hearten, hallow, and protect thee.
Grow'st thou mellow ? What is age ?
Tinct on life's illumined page,
Where the purple letters glow
Deeper, painted long ago.
What is sorrow ? Comfort's prime,
Love's choice Indian summer-clime.
Sickness ? Thou wilt pray it worse
For so blessed, balmy nurse.
And for death ? When thou art dying
'Twill be love beside thee lying.
Death is lonesome ? Oh, how brave
Shows the foot-frequented grave !
Heaven itself is but the casket
For Love's treasure, ere he ask it,
Ere with burning heart he follow,
Piercing through corruption's hollow.
If thou art beloved, oh then
Fear no grief of mortal men !

ONCE, his feet among the roses,
　　When the roses were all white,
Eros wreathed the faint, wan posies
Round Zeus' goblet; but, ere sipping,
'Mid the buds his ankle tripping,
Lavished half the vintage bright
On the roses, that, fresh-dripping,
Flushed the cup for heaven's lipping;
And the god's eyes felt delight
That the roses were not white.

But the sweetest of the roses,
By that fiery rain unfed,
Coyly still her bosom closes,
Still the crimson vesture misses;
Pale 'mid all the purple this is.
Love, thy burning wine-drops shed!
When her blushes make my blisses,
Glowing answer to my kisses,
In thy triumph be it said
That the roses are all red.

L ET us wreathe the mighty cup,
    Then with song we'll lift it up,
And, before we drain the glow
Of the juice that foams below
Flowers and cool leaves round the brim,
Let us swell the praise of him
Who is tyrant of the heart,
Cupid with his flaming dart!

Pride before his face is bowed,
Strength and heedless beauty cowed;
Underneath his fatal wings
Bend discrowned the heads of kings;
Maidens blanch beneath his eye
And its laughing mastery;
Through each land his arrows sound,
By his fetters all are bound.

O WIND, thou hast thy kingdom in the trees,
    And all thy royalties
Sweep through the land to-day.
    It is mid June,
And thou, with all thine instruments in tune,

          Thine orchestra
Of heaving fields, and heavy, swinging fir,
          Strikest a lay
          That doth rehearse
Her ancient freedom to the universe.
      All other sound in awe
          Repeals its law ;
      The bird is mute, the sea
      Sucks up its waves, from rain
      The burthened clouds refrain,
   To listen to thee in thy leafery,
          Thou unconfined,
Lavish, large, soothing, refluent summer-wind !

      DEATH, men say, is like a sea
          That engulfs mortality,
   Treacherous, dreadful, blindingly
          Full of storm and terror.

   Death is like the deep, warm sand
   Pleasant when we come to land,
   Covering up with tender hand
          The wave's drifted error.

Life's a tortured, booming gurge
Winds of passion strike and urge,
And transmute to broken surge
  Foam-crests of ambition.

Death's a couch of golden ground,
Warm, soft, permeable mound,
Where from even memory's sound
  We shall have remission.

AH, Eros doth not always smite
  With cruel, shining dart,
Whose bitter point with sudden might
  Rends the unhappy heart—
Not thus forever purple-stained,
  And sore with steely touch,
Else were its living fountain drained
  Too oft and overmuch.
O'er it sometimes the boy will deign
  Sweep the shaft's feathered end ;
And friendship rises without pain
  Where the white plumes descend.

WHO hath ever given
    Cupid's head white hair,
Or hath put our roses
Under the snow's care?
If such a fool there be
We'll cry him God's mercie!

SOMETIMES I do despatch my heart
    Among the graves to dwell apart:
On some the tablets are erased,
Some earthquake-tumbled, some defaced,
And some that have forgotten lain
A fall of tears makes green again;
And my brave heart can overtread
Her brood of hopes, her infant dead,
And pass with quickened footsteps by
The headstone of hoar memory,
        Till she hath found
        One swelling mound
With just her name writ and *beloved*;
From that she cannot be removed.

DOWN the forest-path I fled,
  And followed a buzzing bee,
Till he clomb a foxglove red.
He filled full the nodding cup;
I stood and I laughed to see;
Then closed it and shut him up,
Till I laughed and set him free.

I DANCE and dance! Another faun,
  A black one, dances on the lawn.
He moves with me, and when I lift
My heels his feet directly shift:
I can't outdance him though I try;
He dances nimbler than I.
I toss my head, and so does he;
What tricks he dares to play on me!
I touch the ivy in my hair;
Ivy he has and finger there.
The spiteful thing to mock me so!
I will outdance him! Ho, ho, ho!

I N the moony brake,
  When we laugh and wake,
And our dance begins,
Violets hang their chins,
      Fast asleep ;
While we laugh and leap.

Woodbine leaves above,
Each a tiny dove,
Roost upon the bare
Winter stems, and there
      Peaceful cling ;
While we shout and sing.

On the rooty earth
Ferns of April's birth,
Brown and closely furled,
Sleep like squirrels curled
      Warm and still ;
While we frisk our fill.

Hark ! our ears have caught
Sound of breath and snort
Near our beechen tree
Mixing carelessly.

    Sprites, away !
Fly as if 'twere day !

*   *   *   *

Silence ! on the ground
Set the toadstool round.
Of these mortals twain
We to talk will deign,
Grave and wise,
Till the morning rise.

L OVE doth never know
   Why it is beloved,
And to ask were treason:
   Let the wonder grow !
Were its hopes removed,
Were itself disproved
   By cold reason,
In its happy season
Love would be beloved.

SWEET Love, awake! You must be
        singing;
  Put all your deadly darts away;
Pass through the woods; your voice's ringing
        Alone will slay.
Sweet Love, with your sweet music fill us;
Without a weapon you will kill us.

MEN, looking on the Wandering Jew,
        Straightway must flee him;
My love each mortal must pursue
    Soon as they see him.
I would my love immortal grew,
Winning shy women's hearts to woo;
I from my grave would listen too,
    Would bless and free him.

LOVE'S wings are wondrous swift
        When hanging feathers lift.
    Why hath Love wings,
Great pinions strong of curve?
His wild desires to serve;
    To swoop on the prey,
    And bear it away,
        Love hath wings.

Love's wings are golden soft,
When dropping from aloft.
   Why hath Love wings,
Feathers of glistening fleece?
To soothe with balmy peace,
   And warmth of his breath
   Souls he cherisheth
      Love hath wings.

Love's wings are broad of van,
Stretched for great travel's span.
   Why hath Love wings,
Mail of the sea-bird's might?
From feeble hearts and slight
   To lift him forlorn
   To a fastness of scorn,
      Love hath wings.

IF the sun our white headlands with flame
         Failed to greet,
Should we deem he would shroud them in
      shame?
            Nay, blot
            The sweet

Daylight not:
Heaven forgot.

If soft spring failed the flowers name by name
To entreat,
Should we fear she would harden earth's frame?
Her hot
Breath sweet
Bloweth not;
She forgot.

From my love if no gay token came,
Were it meet
To think she had slighted love's claim?
A knot
So sweet
Snappeth not;
She forgot.

If a land full of memories and fame
At the feet
Of a tyrant bowed down, should we blame?
A spot
So sweet
Sinneth not;
It forgot.

WHEN I grow old,
    I would be bold
To ask of heaven this boon :
Like the thin-circled and translucent moon,
    That makes intrusion
  Unnoted on the morning sky,
    And with soft eye
Watches the thousand, grassy flowers unfold,
    I would be free,
    Without confusion
    Of influence cold,
    To pause and see
The flush of youth in its felicity.

AN APPLE-FLOWER

I FELT my leaves fall free,
  I felt the wind and sun,
At my heart a honey-bee :
  And life was done.

A CALM in the flitting sky,
  And in the calm a moon,
  A youngling golden :
'Mid windy shades an olden

Oak-tree whose branches croon
As the orb sails by.
Heigh ho !
Youth and age, the soft and dry,
While breezes blow.

Its crookèd arm the oak
Points upward to the moon ;
A sapless member,
Which scorching of November
And levin shafts of June
In their season broke.
Heigh ho !
Age is gruff with blight and stroke,
While breezes blow.

But storm has left no trace
Upon the blithe new moon,
That westward slideth,
And on the white wind rideth :
It does not weary soon
Of the blowing race.
Heigh ho !
Youth is free and sweet of face,
While breezes blow.

BUTTERFLY bright,
   Thou dost alight
On the sunflower-bed;
For the nectar sunny
   Thou div'st, drinking dumb:
   While the bee instead,
   With a laboured hum,
Clogs and soils himself with the honey.

   A blessèd thing
   To poise and cling
Mid the sweets without
A thought of the morrow,
   To quaff and to bask,
   While the busy rout
   Grows dull at its task
Of heaping up riches and sorrow.

   Oh, let me be
   That creature, free
From thought of the hive,
That doth never stint her
   Gay soul of its fill;
   But warm and alive
   Feeds, feeding until
The fall of the leaf and the winter!

SO jealous of your beauty,
  You will not wed
    For dread
That hymeneal duty
  Should touch and mar
The lovely thing you are ?
Come to your garden-bed!

Learn there another lesson :
  This poppy-head,
    Instead
Of having crimson dress on,
  Is now a fruit,
Whose marvellous pale suit
Transcends the glossy red.

What, count the colour
  Of apricot,
    Ungot,
Warming in August, duller
  Than those most shy,
Frail flowers that spread and die
Before the sun is hot !

Lady, the hues unsightly,
  And best forgot,
    Are not
Berries and seeds set brightly,
  But withered blooms :
  Alack, vainglory dooms
You to their ragged lot !

I N winter sere,
    We little men o' the hill
No longer duck and peer
Up holy daffodil,
  Nor suck the egg
  That the cuckoo lays,
  Nor the angry leg
  Of the chafer wring
  Till the gray-pate sing
  With his stiff amaze :
  No, no, no, no !
To keep ourselves warm in row
We run—ta, la, la, lo !

  A valley's end
Is steep and flat at the top,

No pathways there may wend
Across the sweet-fern crop,
   As dead as straw;
   At the sign-post wry
   All the winds see-saw,
   And with chilly feet
   We little ones meet
   On the rim of sky.
   We start, stay, go,
And down to the pool below
We run—ta, la, la, lo!

THROUGH hazels and apples
   My love I led,
Where the sunshine dapples
   The strawberry-bed:
Did we pluck and eat
   That morn, my sweet?

And back by the alley
   Our path I chose,
That we might dally
   By one rare rose:

Did we smell at the heart,
   And then depart?

A lover, who grapples
   With love, doth live
Where roses and apples
   Have naught to give:
Did I take my way
   Unfed that day?

SAY, if a gallant rose my bower doth scale,
   Higher and higher,
And, tho' she twine the other side the pale,
   Toward me doth sigh her
  Perfume, her damask mouth—
  Roses will love the south—
   Can I deny her?

I have a lady loves me in despite
   Of bonds that tie her,
And bid her honest Corin's flame requite;
   When I espy her,
  Kisses are near their birth—
  Love cannot live in dearth—
   Say, shall I fly her?

IF Dahlia died I could not weep,
    It were to look on Death asleep:
In Dahlia's arms to die would be
A perfect immortality.

LOVE rises up some days
    From a blue couch of light
    Upon the summer sky;
He wakes, and waking plays
With beams and dewdrops white;
His laugh is like the sunniest rain,
    And patters through his voice;
He is so lovely, tolerant, and sane,
    That the heart questions why
It doth not, every hour it beats, rejoice.

Yet sometimes Love awakes
On a black, hellish bed,
    And rises up as hate:
He drinks the hurtful lakes,
He joys to toss and spread
Sparkles of pitchy, rankling flame,
    He joys to play with death;

But when we look on him he is the same
    Quaint child we blest of late,
And every word that once he said he saith.

AH me, if I grew sweet to man
    It was but as a rose that can
No longer keep the breath that heaves
And swells among its folded leaves.

The pressing fragrance would unclose
The flower, and I became a rose,
That unimpeachable and fair
Planted an odour in the air.

No art I used men's love to draw;
I lived but by my being's law,
As roses are by heaven designed
To bring the honey to the wind.

I found there is scant sun in spring,
I found the blast a riving thing;
Yet even ruined roses can
No other than be sweet to man.

WHERE winds abound,
    And fields are hilly,
Shy daffadilly
Looks down on the ground.

Rose cones of larch
Are just beginning ;
Though oaks are spinning
No oak-leaves in March.

Spring's at the core,
The boughs are sappy :
Good to be happy
So long, long before !

THE SECOND BOOK OF SONGS

THE TABLE OF THE SECOND BOOK

THE SECOND BOOK OF SONGS

SLOWLY we disarray,
    Our leaves grow few,
Few on the bough, and many on the sod :
Round him no ruining autumn tempest blew ;
    Gathered on genial day,
    He fills, fresh as Apollo's bay,
        The Hand of God.

I STOOD to hear that bold
    Sentence of grit and mould,
    Earth to earth ; they thrust
    On his coffin dust ;
Stones struck against his grave :
O the old days, the brave !

Just with a pebble's fall,
Grave-digger, you turn all
    Bliss to bereaving ;
    To catch the cleaving

Of Atropa's fine shears
Would less hurt human ears.

Live senses that death dooms!
For friendship in dear rooms,
  Slow-lighting faces,
  Hand-clasps, embraces,
Ashes on ashes grind:
O poor lips left behind!

Mortality turns round
On mortals in that sound:
  Ears are for the knell
  Of a muffled bell:
Touch, for clods of earth;
Sight, for torture and dearth.

OTHERS may drag at memory's fetter,
  May turn for comfort to the vow
Of mortal breath; I hold it better
To learn if verily and how
Love knits me with the loved one now.

Others for solace, sleep-forsaken,
May muse upon the days of old;
To me it is delight to waken,
To find my Dead, to feel them fold
My heart, and for its dross give gold.

B RING me life of fickle breath,
    Bring me death;
Summon every hope's alloy;
Gather round me what doth most
    Love to boast
That it can our bliss deflower!
There is now no mortal power
That can feed upon my joy;
Every terror is o'erthrown:
I have found the magic stone,
For a dead heart is my own.

Henceforth is it not pure gold
    To grow old?
Let the hours of parting fleet!
While to think of what befell
    Is to dwell
At the mouth o' the honeycomb
Where the soul-bee hath its home,

Where the soul-bee hives its sweet.
And the heaven to come at last !
Bravely may I now forecast
Since I hold the loved one fast.

AH me, how sadder than to say farewell
        It is to meet
Dreading that Love hath lost his spell
        And changed his sweet !
I would we were again to part,
        With that full heart.

The hawthorn was half-bud, half-flower,
        At our goodbye ;
And braver to me since that hour
        Are earth and sky :
My God, it were too poor a thing
        To meet this spring.

Our hearts—life never would have marge
        To bear their tides,
Their confluent rush ! Lo, death is large
        In boundary-sides ;
And our great χαῖρε must be said
        When I am dead.

DEATH, for all thy grasping stealth,
    Thou dost convey
Lands to us of broadest wealth,
    That stretch away
Where the sunshine hath no foil,
Past the verge of our dark soil,
Past the rim where clouds uncoil.

Mourners, whom thine avarice dooms,
    Once given a space
In thy kingdom past the tombs,
    With open face
See the smallness of our skies,
Large, until a mortal dies
And shrinks them to created size.

O the freedom, that doth spread,
    When life is shown
The great countries that the dead
    Have open thrown ;
Where, at our best leisure, we
With a spirit may walk free
From terrestrial poverty.

LITTLE Lettuce is dead, they say,
  The brown, sweet child who rolled in
      the hay;
  Ah, where shall we find her?
  For the neighbours pass
  To the pretty lass,
In a linen cere-cloth to wind her.

If her sister were set to search
The nettle-green nook beside the church,
    And the way were shown her
    Through the coffin-gate
    To her dead playmate,
She would fly too frighted to own her.

Should she come at a noonday call,
Ah, stealthy, stealthy, with no footfall,
    And no laughing chatter,
    To her mother 'twere worse
    Than a barren curse
That her own little wench should pat her.

Little Lettuce is dead and gone!
The stream by her garden wanders on

Through the rushes wider ;
She fretted to know
How its bright drops grow
On the hills, but no hand would guide her.

Little Lettuce is dead and lost !
Her willow-tree boughs by storm are tossed—
    O the swimming sallows !—
    Where she crouched to find
    The nest of the wind
Like a water-fowl's in the shallows.

Little Lettuce is out of sight !
The river-bed and the breeze are bright :
    Ay me, were it sinning
    To dream that she knows
    Where the soft wind rose
That her willow-branches is thinning ?

Little Lettuce has lost her name,
Slipt away from our praise and our blame;
    Let not love pursue her,
    But conceive her free
    Where the bright drops be
On the hills, and no longer rue her !

SOLITARY Death, make me thine own,
   And let us wander the bare fields
      together;
   Yea, thou and I alone,
Roving in unembittered unison forever.

   I will not harry thy treasure-graves,
I do not ask at thy still hands a lover;
      My heart within me craves
To travel till we twain Time's wilderness
      discover.

   To sojourn with thee my soul was bred,
And I, the courtly sights of life refusing,
      To the wide shadows fled,
And mused upon thee often as I fell a-musing.

   Escaped from chaos, thy mother Night,
In her maiden breast a burthen that awed her,
      By cavern waters white
Drew thee her first-born, her unfathered off-
      spring, toward her.

   On dewy plats, near twilight dingle,
She oft, to still thee from men's sobs and curses

In thine ears a-tingle,
Pours her cool charms, her weird, reviving
chaunt rehearses.

Though mortals menace thee or elude,
And from thy confines break in swift trans-
gression.
Thou for thyself art sued
Of me, I claim thy cloudy purlieus my
possession.

To a lone freshwater, where the sea
Stirs the silver flux of the reeds and willows,
Come thou, and beckon me
To lie in the lull of the sand-sequestered
billows:

Then take the life I have called my own
And to the liquid universe deliver;
Loosening my spirit's zone,
Wrap round me as thy limbs the wind, the
light, the river.

A DEATH-BED

HER husband kept
Watch by her side; no word she spoke

Of parting ; but the children crept
To bid good-night : she slept,
And, sleeping, never woke.

O TIME, of man little but blame thou
     gainest :
  I will not chide thy name, but praise,
  Seeing that my harsh, unhappy days
  Thou dost restore me changed and mellow,
As when the sun turns stony marbles yellow.

Thou in a thousand, tender ways revivest ;
  Thou givest nothing that is crude,
  Sweetening from beds of solitude
  Thy stores as from a bed of spices.
O Time, thy subtle touch beyond all price is !

Laden with more, more blessing thou arrivest,
  With promise of such gifts to come,
  If ever yesterday's full sum
  Should be without a break completed
Eternity itself would be firm-seated.

For us with life's unnumbered hues thou
      stainest
  Oblivion, till it come to pass
  We see it through a coloured glass :
  Nor can we love thee less that in abiding
Retreats thou hast the Muses safe in hiding

B URY her at even,
    That the stars may shine
  Soon above her,
And the dews of twilight cover :
  Bury her at even,
  Ye that love her.

Bury her at even,
At the shut of flowers
  Softly take her ;
They will lie beside nor wake her :
  Bury her at even
  At the shut of flowers.

Bury her at even
In the wind's decline ;
  Night receive her

Where no noise may ever grieve her !
  Bury her at even,
  And then leave her !

I BY spells had been beguiled
  To a marish country wild,
Where a lonely-hearted child
Crossed me ; and I felt she knew
All the way she wandered through,
Though the reeds around her blew,
And the dusk was in her rear,
As I watched her disappear
'Mid the flitting umbrage drear.

YONDER slope of sunny ground
  One day by a fence was bound ;
First it felt within its soil
Digging mortals sing and toil ;
Then a weight was lowered deep,
And the grave became a heap
On an earth that only knew
What it was to feed on dew ;
Zephyr touched its wayward flowers,
Birds had tripped on it for hours,

Life, she spun its grass intact,
Till Death wrought the delver's act.

Now no more the sunny slope
Lies in its own bloom and hope,
For an alien power destroys
Its unheedful, perfect joys.
Mortals dig at night and noon,
Grave near grave is huddled soon;
While across the jocund grass
Doom and lamentation pass:
Sorrow lingers round the place.
Innocent of drear disgrace,
It had lived beneath no blame
When but birds and zephyr came.

Youth—ah, youth, it is a field
We would never, never yield
To intrusion of the grave,
'Tis an acre we would save!
Yet one day a mound we see
Breaking its stability,
And the knowledge that is strange
Hath begun to spoil and change
Sweetness that was never bred

From remembrance of the dead,
But by nature had been sown,
As are greeny banks unmown.

One by one the tombs are pressed
In the boundaries of our breast ;
Every year the native charm
Of our being suffers harm ;
What it had not held before
It must cherish more and more,
Till we scarcely breathe a breath
That is ignorant of death ;
For our flowers as we grow old,
Saddened, live on burial mould,
And the earth in us is made
Fruitful by the sexton's spade.

A CURLING thread
　Uncoils overhead—
From the chimney-stack
A replenished track
Of vapour, in haste
To increase and waste,
Growing wings as it grows
Of amber and rose,

With an upward flight
To the frosty light.
Puff on puff
Of the soft breath-stuff,
Till the cloudy fleece
Thickens its feathers; its rounds increase,
Mingle and widen, and lose the line
Of their dull confine,
Thinning mote by mote
As they upward float,
And by-and-bye
Are effaced on the sky.

To evoke,
Like the smoke,
Dower on dower
By the power
Of our art:
To have part
In the air and the sun,
Till our course be run,
Till the sigh be breathed,
Till the wreath be wreathed,
And we disappear,
Leaving heaven clear!

SHE mingled me rue and roses,
    And I found my bliss complete :
    The roses are gone,
    But the rue lives on,
The bitter that lived with the sweet.

Life will mingle you rue and roses ;
The roses will fall at your feet :
    But deep in the rue
    That their leaves bestrew
The bitter will smell of the sweet.

I WOULD not die
    To meet a goodly company ;
I was ever, ever shy,
And have loved to live retired,
That I might con
Some mystery scarce pondered on.
Oh, this I have desired !

No hope to brood
Where harpers wing on wing intrude,
Or bold saints with trumpets rude ;

Where four beasts from turning eyne
Watch my strange ways :
But in concealment of deep rays
May some recess be mine!

I never can,
On earth, though quite escaped from man,
Put society under ban :
Buzzing bees swing in a flower,
Gnats drum and dance,
The weasel intercepts my trance,
Birds warble through a bower.

Once Chloe graced
My suit; how fondly we embraced!
Still my arm was round her waist:
Chloe dropt her pretty head
Upon my knee,
And Love was left alone with me
Just while she slumberèd.

And once I lay
In sickness; I had swooned away,
For I wandered as at play;

It was untethered innocence :
Naught of my own
I had, the night was open thrown,
Sound wrought no more offence.

Endowed by thee,
Death, let me enter privacy,
Unmorose and fellowly
To mix, with the free pleasure
Of stars and springs
And magic, unfamiliar things,
My beauteous leisure.

WHEN thou to death, fond one, wouldst
        fain be starting,
    I did not pray
    That thou shouldst stay;
    Alone I lay
And dreamed and wept and watched thee on
        thy way.

But now thou dost return, yea, after parting,
        And me embrace,
        Our souls enlace;

Ask thou no grace;
Thou shalt be aye confinèd to this place.

*   *   *   *   *

Alone, alone I lie, ah, bitter smarting!
    Thou to the last
    Didst cling, kiss fast,
    Yet art thou past
Beyond me, in the hollow of a blast.

IS it the sun
    Quickens athwart these leaves of vine
A blush of redder stain than wine?
    One after one,
    Is it the light
    That loves and reaches
    The mantling peaches,
    With vigour bright?
    And is it life
    Which thus is rife
Through all the wane and shadow of thy face,
    In autumn grace?

    Nay, 'tis the frost
Makes the best colour of the year:

E

The vine-leaves deep as grapes appear
  Where rime has crossed;
  It is the cold
  That strikes with glory
  Of crimson hoary
  The peaches' mould;
  Yea, it is death
  Whose bracing breath
Illumes thy cheek with more than nuptial rush
  Of ripened flush.

THERE is a fair, white relic in my room:
  God, how I love it!
   Twine, twine
  Green keys of sycamine
  Round and above it,
Then lay it softly in my heart's new tomb.

Ah, mourning friends, these sullen sighs and
   deep
  No longer breathe me!
   Sing, sing
  Praise of the royal thing
  Death doth bequeath me,
And carve me in my memory to keep!

VAIN Death, thou hast no staying,
　Thou dost not lag behind
Dear Life in thy decaying;
　An instant thou dost claim
　My Dahlia's frame;
But this corruption that men call thy preying
　Is love that blows thee to the wind.

DREAM not no darkness bars
　Her world, who in the stars
　　Had such delight
That jealously she turned to slumber;
Her eyelids now sleep doth not cumber,
　And she, awake all night,
　Helps God to number
　　The shining stars.

NO longer will she bend
　Her fine, pale face o'er any,
A benediction spend
That was a faith to many:
　For like the moon, her face
With God's great sunlight shone,
　Mellowed in grace

That the weak-eyed might look upon
 Life, and be glad;
She kept mid cloudy hearts a gracious place,
 So much of day she had.

 Emotions deep she swayed
With beautiful, swift stillness;
 The world of waves obeyed
Her beck in wane and illness;
 She drew them to a shore,
She carried them aloft
 With strenuous lore
So secretly that oft
 Men could not guess
It was her influence, elect and soft,
 Moved through the sea to bless.

 Yet in unfounded sky
She had her nearest pleasure;
 She loved to travel high
On space no rod can measure:
 Remote she dwelt from speech,
And though her path, her goal
 But few could reach,
Her lonely, glowing soul

Ruled from its height
Secure, so courteously she offered each
  Her fount of golden light.

I LAID her to sleep,
  And I came to weep
By her forest-grave; but I found
  That a squirrel gay
  At its noiseless play
Was springing across the mound.

  The sun made a mote
  Of gold on its coat,
On its pretty hind-legs it stood;
  Then without a sound
  Leapt·over the mound
To its home again in the wood.

WINDS to-day are large and free,
  Winds to-day are westerly;
From the land they seem to blow
Whence the sap begins to flow
And the dimpled light to spread,
From the country of the dead.

Ah, it is a wild, sweet land
Where the coming May is planned,
Where such influences throb
As our frosts can never rob
Of their triumph, when they bound
Through the tree and from the ground.

Great within me is my soul,
Great to journey to its goal,
To the country of the dead;
For the cornel-tips are red,
And a passion rich in strife
Drives me toward the home of life.

Oh, to keep the spring with them
Who have flushed the cornel-stem,
Who imagine at its source
All the year's delicious course,
Then express by wind and light
Something of their rapture's height!

UNCONSCIOUSNESS.

HE with the Gentle Ones is hid from sight:
We may not follow. He hath dwelt
with woes

So dread, he lays his confidence in those
Men shrink from, who remember and requite.
O comfort him, sweet daughters of the Night,
For fear of whom man's thought doth softly
      tread;
Within your grove let him be deeply led
To reconciliation and repose.

H OW rapidly the land
    With spring's fresh current fills,
And all its summer bravery discloses!
The stubborn apple-trees alone resist,
Nor will relax a muscle of the twist
    In their gnarled maze;
Their sappy veins some crabbèd hindrance
      dams:
    Hoar lichen grays
Their budless boughs; they stand
Like grave-plots mid the pleasant garden-hills,
  O'erset with starry primroses,
    And blissful lambs.

A S dust on a cloudy, summer day
  Covers the lilies with sordid gray,

So, your disdaining
The pureness of my love is staining.

Perfume, splendour there is in my breast,
Crystal and gold.   Do you pass and jest?
    Look backward, scoffer!
No more that candour bright I proffer.

O cruel sin, thus to blotch with scorn
A joy of morning and heaven just born;
    First to acquaint me
With love, and then assoil and taint me.

O LOVE, remember that your eyes
    Will crumble into dust;
Remember that with me it lies
    Indignantly to thrust
Corruption from the things I praise,
Or from their very earth to raise
Such fair and living forms that men
Will feel their beauty born again.

But, while I give you endless life,
    A living death you dole,

Consuming me with mortal strife,
  Dragging my weary soul
Through haunted shadows, where decay
Creeps over peace, where day by day
Old joys are ravaged in my heart,
Whence fixedness and pride depart.

I give you life, you give me death;
  We could not take nor give
Except that you are drawing breath
  Just when I chance to live :
Cursed be this little ell of time !
Oh, are not Fate's awards sublime !
My love will keep your beauty brave,
Long after you have dug my grave.

THEY say my love to death is sick ;
  I hear the news, my heart beats quick,
And then grows dumb and dumber ;
For if on him the earth must lie,
The sunshine will no more pass by ;
'Tis not a summer that will die,
  But summer.

While poets on the earth still rove
He must be there to feed their love,
His breath such breath infuses ;
And if it fail, the gods destroy
Not just a lurid, lovely boy,
But rather, with the Muses' joy,
    The Muses.

PINK and fresh,
   In a mesh
Shake them down !
The deep, budding roses,
Ere evening closes,
   Will be brown.

Love will stay
Just its day
Like a bloom :
But the love I cherish
Shall change, shall perish
   On his tomb.

WHEN the cherries are on the bough
   To my lips I raise them ;

But now, ah now
The best I can do is to praise them,
And to think all through November
Of the brightest I remember.

When the roses are opening, how
I stoop down to kiss them;
But now, ah now
By the empty rose-bush I miss them,
And I dream all through November
Of the sweetest I remember.

The birds still sing on the bough,
They love without mating;
But now, ah now,
No warmth of the spring they are waiting,
For they sing all through November
Of the April they remember.

THANATOS, thy praise I sing,
Thou immortal, youthful king!
Glorious offerings I will bring;
For men say thou hast no shrine,
And I find thou art divine

As no other god: thy rage
Doth preserve the Golden Age,
What we blame is thy delay :
Cut the flowers ere they decay !

Come, we would not derogate,
Age and nipping pains we hate,
Take us at our best estate :
While the head burns with the crown,
In the battle strike us down !
At the bride-feast do not think
From thy summons we should shrink ;
We would give our latest kiss
To a life still warm with bliss.

Come and take us to thy train
Of dead maidens on the plain
Where white lilies have no stain ;
Take us to the youths, that thou
Lov'st to choose, of fervid brow,
Unto whom thy dreaded name
Hath been simply known as Fame :
With these unpolluted things
Be our endless revellings.

THE THIRD BOOK OF SONGS

TABLE OF THE THIRD BOOK

THE THIRD BOOK OF SONGS

WHEN high Zeus first peopled earth,
     As sages say,
All were children of one birth,
Helpless nurslings.   Doves and bees
Tended their soft infancies:
Hand to hand they tossed the ball,
And none smiled to see the play,
    Nor stood aside
      In pride
And pleasure of their youthful day.
    All waxed gray,
Mourning in companies the winter dearth:
  Whate'er they saw befall
  Their neighbours, they
  Felt in themselves; so lay
    On life a pall.

Zeus at the confusion smiled,
    And said, " From hence
Man by change must be beguiled;

F

Age with royalties of death,
Childhood, sweeter than its breath,
Will be won, if we provide
Generation's difference."
    Wisely he planned ;
    The tiny hand,
In eld's weak palm found providence,
  And each through influence
Of things beholden and not borne grew mild :
  Youths by the old man's side
    Their turbulence
    To crystal sense
    Saw clarified.

Dear, is not the story's truth
    Most manifest ?
Had our lives been twinned, forsooth,
We had never had one heart :
By time set a space apart,
We are bound by such close ties
None can tell of either breast
    The native sigh
      Who try
To learn with whom the Muse is guest.
  How sovereignly I'm blest

To see and smell the rose of my own youth
  In thee : how pleasant lies
      My life, at rest
From dream, its hope expressed
      Before mine eyes.

ALREADY to mine eyelids' shore
      The gathering waters swell,
For thinking of the grief in store
  When thou wilt say " Farewell."
I dare not let thee leave me, sweet,
  Lest it should be for ever ;
Tears dew my kisses ere we meet,
  Foreboding we must sever :
Since we can neither meet nor part,
Methinks the moral is, sweetheart,
  That we must dwell together.

COWSLIP-GATHERING

TWAIN cannot mingle : we went hand in
      hand,
Yearning, divided, through the fair spring
      land,

Nor knew, twin maiden spirits, there must be
In all true marriage perfect trinity.
But lo! dear Nature spied us, in a copse
Filling with chirps of song and hazel-drops,
And smiled : " These children I will straight
       espouse,
While the blue cuckoo thrills the alder-boughs."
So led us to a tender, marshy nook
Of meadow-verdure, where by twos and threes
The cowslips grew, down-nodding toward a
      brook;
And left us there to pluck them at our ease
In the moist quiet, till the rich content
Of the bee humming in the cherry-trees
Filled us; in one our very being blent.

A GIRL,
    Her soul a deep-wave pearl
Dim, lucent of all lovely mysteries;
  A face flowered for heart's ease,
  A brow's grace soft as seas
  Seen through faint forest-trees :
  A mouth, the lips apart,
Like aspen-leaflets trembling in the breeze

From her tempestuous heart.
Such: and our souls so knit,
I leave a page half-writ—
      The work begun
Will be to heaven's conception done,
      If she come to it.

M ETHINKS my love to thee doth grow,
         And this the sign:
  I see the Spirit claim thee,
  And do not blame thee,
Nor break intrusive on the Holy Ground
  Where thou of God art found.

      I watch the fire
  Leap up, and do not bring
  Fresh water from the spring
To keep it from up-flaming higher
  Than my chilled hands require
      For cherishing.

I see thy soul turn to her hidden grot,
      And follow not;

Content thou shouldst prefer
    To be with her,
The heavenly Muse, than ever find in me
    Best company.

So brave my love is grown,
I joy to find thee sought
    By some great thought;
And am content alone
To eat life's common fare,
    While thou prepare
To be my royal moment's guest :
    Live to the Best!

Τοῖς μὲν ἀοιδὰς, τοῖς δ' αὖ δακρύων
Βίον ἀμβλωπὸν παρέχουσαι.

APOLLO and the Muses taught thee not
  Thy mighty strain, enchantment to the
    mind,
Thralling the heart by spell of holy fears;
Awful thou sought'st Erinys' sacred grot;
And the Eternal Goddess, well-inclin'd,
Hath given thee songs, for the dull life of
    tears.

IF I but dream that thou art gone,
  My heart aches to o'ertake thee;
How shall I then forsake thee
    In clear daylight,
Who art my very joy's nativity—
Thee, whose sweet soul I con
    Secure to find
    Perfect epitome
Of nature, passion, poesy?
    From thee untwined,
I shall but wander a disbodied sprite,
    Until thou wake me
With thy kiss-warmèd breath, and take me
    Where we are one.

A SPRING MORNING BY THE SEA

I DID not take me to the sea,
  When the winged morning wakened me
With beamy plumes: I used them right
To bear me in an Eastern flight
Of arrowy swiftness to the bed
Where my beloved still slumberèd,
Lying half poet and half child,

The twin divineness reconciled.
And I, who scarce could breathe to see
Her spirit in its secrecy
So innocent, drew back in awe
That I should give such creature law;
Then looked and found God standing near,
And to His Rule resigned my Dear.

KING APOLLO

WHEN my lady sleeping lies,
Her sweet breaths her lips unbar ;
This when King Apollo spies,
With dream footfall, not to mar
The dear sleep,
Through the rosy doors ajar
He with golden thoughts doth creep.

LOVE'S SOUR LEISURE

AS a poem in my mind
Thy sweet lineaments are shrined :
From the memory, alas !
Sweetest, sweetest verse will pass ;
And the fragments I must piece

Lest the fair tradition cease.
There is balmy air I trow
On the uplands of thy brow,
But the temple's veinèd mound
Is the Muses' sacred ground;
While the tresses pale are groves
That the laurelled godhead loves.
There is something in the cheek
Like a dimple still to seek,
As my poet timidly
Love's incarnate kiss would flee.
But the mouth! That land to own
Long did Aphroditè moan,
Ere the virgin goddess grave
From the temptress of the wave
That most noble clime did win;
Who, retreating to the chin,
Took her boy's bow for a line,
The sweet boundary to define,
And about the beauteous bays
Still in orbèd queenship plays.
I have all the charaçt'ry
Of thy features, yet lack thee;
And by couplets to confess
What I wholly would possess

Doth but whet the appetite
Of my too long-famished sight:
Vainly if my eyes entreat,
Tears will be their daily meat.

I SING thee with the stock-dove's throat,
　Warm, crooning, superstitious note,
That on its dearie so doth dote
　　It falls to sorrow,
And from the fair, white swans afloat
　　A dirge must borrow.

In thee I have such deep content,
I can but murmur a lament;
It is as though my heart were rent
　　By thy perfection,
And all my passion's torrent spent
　　In recollection.

ACHERON

ELAIA, my soul's bride,
　Thou must not leave me!
Though 'tis a mournful land

Through which I travel,
I will but take thee by the hand,
   And be thy guide
To mysteries thou must in art unravel.
When thou a little way art gone,
Ere the grove's steep descent
Darkening can grieve thee,
Thou backward to the sweet stars shalt be sent;
   While I plod on
   To Acheron.

NO beauty born of pride my lady hath;
   Her voice is as the path
Of a sweet stream, and where it flows must be
   Peace and fertility.
Who loveth her no tumult hath or pain;
Her cloudy eyes are full of blessèd rain,
   A sky that cherisheth; her breast
   Is a soft nook for rest.
   She hath no varying pleasure
   For passion's fitful mood;
Her firm, small kisses are my constant food,
As rowan-berries yield their treasure

To starving birds; her smile
Gives life so sweet a style,
To die beneath its beams would be
To practise immortality.

M Y lady hath a lovely rite:
      When I am gone
No prayer she saith
As one in fear:
For orison,
Pressing her pillow white
With kisses, just the sacred number,
She turns to slumber;
Adding sometimes thereto a tear
And a quick breath.

M Y love is like a lovely shepherdess;
      She has a dress
         Of peach and green,
The prettiest was ever seen:
         All eyes must bless
The passing of my pretty shepherdess.

My love is like the first day of the spring,
      To everything
      She gives a grace,
  Touching it with her tender face:
      Ye lambkins cling
To her, and frolic in the sunshining!

My love is like the earliest streak of morn,
      Ere day is born;
      So virgin white,
  The sun with his transfiguring light
      Fears to adorn
That tremulous, pellucid streak of morn.

O love, O springtime, morning shepherdess,
      Of my distress
      I tell my flute;
  To thee I must be ever mute,
      And, weeping, bless
The footprints of my sacred shepherdess.

UNBOSOMING

THE love that breeds
  In my heart for thee!
As the iris is full, brimful of seeds,

And all that it flowered for among the reeds
Is packed in a thousand vermilion-beads
That push, and riot, and squeeze, and clip,
Till they burst the sides of the silver scrip,
And at last we see
What the bloom, with its tremulous, bowery
    fold
Of zephyr-petal at heart did hold:
So my breast is rent
With the burthen and strain of its great
    content;
For the summer of fragrance and sighs is dead,
The harvest-secret is burning red,
And I would give thee, after my kind,
The final issues of heart and mind.

A GRAY mob-cap and a girl's
    Soft circle of sprouting curls,
That proclaim she has had the fever:
How dear the days when the child was nurst!
My God, I pray she may die the first,
    That I may not leave her!

Her head on my knee laid down,
That *duvet* so warm, so brown,
I fondle, I dote on its springing.
" Thou must never grow lonesome or old,
Leave me rather to darkness and cold,
　　O my Life, my Singing ! "

IT was deep April, and the morn
　　Shakspere was born;
The world was on us, pressing sore ;
My Love and I took hands and swore,
　Against the world, to be
Poets and lovers evermore,
To laugh and dream on Lethe's shore,
To sing to Charon in his boat,
Heartening the timid souls afloat ;
Of judgment never to take heed,
But to those fast-locked souls to speed,
Who never from Apollo fled,
Who spent no hour among the dead ;
　　Continually
　　With them to dwell,
Indifferent to heaven and hell.

THERE comes a change in her breath,
    A change that saith
She is breathing in her sleep,
Breathing, breathing and yet so low :
O life at ebb, O life at flow,
    Her life, her breath !

AN INVITATION

COME and sing, my room is south ;
    Come, with thy sun-governed mouth,
Thou wilt never suffer drouth,
    Long as dwelling
In my chamber of the south.

On the wall there is woodbine,
With its yellow-scarlet shine ;
When my lady's hopes decline,
    Honey-smelling
Trumpets will her mood divine.

There are myrtles in a row ;
Lady, when the flower's in blow,
Kisses passing to and fro,
    From our smelling,
Think, what lovely dreams will grow !

There's a lavender settee,
Cushioned for my sweet and me;
Ah, what secrets there will be
    For love-telling,
When her head leans on my knee!

Books I have of long ago
And to-day; I shall not know
Some, unless thou read them, so
    Their excelling
Music needs thy voice's flow:

Campion, with a noble ring
Of choice spirits; count this wing
Sacred! all the songs I sing
    Welling, welling
From Elizabethan spring:

French, that corner of primrose!
Flaubert, Verlaine, with all those
Precious, little things in prose,
    Bliss-compelling,
Howsoe'er the story goes:

G

All the Latins *thou* dost prize!
Cynthia's lover by thee lies;
Note Catullus, type and size
  Least repelling
To thy weariable eyes.

And for Greek!   Too sluggishly
Thou dost toil; but Sappho, see!
And the dear Anthology
  For thy spelling.
Come, it shall be well with thee.

THE FOURTH BOOK OF SONGS

THE TABLE OF THE FOURTH BOOK

THE FOURTH BOOK OF SONGS

OUR myrtle is in flower ;
    Behold Love's power !
The glorious stamens' crowded force unfurled,
    Cirque beyond cirque
At breathing, bee-like, and harmonious work ;
The rose-patched petals backward curled,
    Falling away
To let fecundity have perfect play.

  O flower, dear to the eyes
    Of Aphrodite, rise
As she at once to bare, audacious bliss;
    And bid us near
Your prodigal, delicious hemisphere,
Where thousand kisses breed the kiss
    That fills the room
With languor of an acid, dark perfume !

I LIVE in the world for his sake,
   For the eyes that sleep and wake,
I live in the world for his eyes :
Earth's kingdoms may pass away,
I heed not these things of clay,
But I live, I love, I pray
   From the light of his eyes.

A CROSS a gaudy room
   I looked and saw his face,
Beneath the sapless palm-trees, in the gloom
   Of the distressing place,
   Where everyone sat tired,
   Where talk itself grew stale,
Where, as the day began to fail,
No guest had just the power required
To rise and go : I strove with my disgust ;
But at the sight of him my eyes were fired
To give one glance, as though they must
Be sociable with what they found of fair
And free and simple in a chamber where
         Life was so base.

   As when a star is lit
   In the dull, evening sky,

Another soon leaps out to answer it,
    Even so the bright reply
    Came sudden from his eyes,
    By all but me unseen;
Since then the distance that between
    Our lives unalterably lies
Is but a darkness, intimate and still,
Which messages may traverse, where replies
    May sparkle from afar, until
The night becomes a mystery made clear
Between two souls forbidden to draw near:
      Creator, why?

GO to the grave,
    Die, die—be dead!
If a Judgment-Angel came and said
    That I could save
My heart and brain, if I could but will
For a single moment that you should die,
I would clasp my hands, and wish you ill,
    And say goodbye.

    Go to the grave,
    Die, die—be dead!

If the Judgment-Angel came and said
    That I could save
My body and soul, if I could but will
For as long as an hour that you should die,
My hands would drop, and my eyes would fill,
    And the angel fly.

A S two fair vessels side by side,
        No bond had tied
    Our floating peace;
We thought that it would never cease,
But like swan-creatures we should always glide:
    And this is love
        We sighed.

As two grim vessels side by side,
        Through wind and tide
        War grappled us,
With bond as strong as death, and thus
We drove on mortally allied:
    And this is hate
        We cried.

O WEEP!
    The lake is icy, and the rim
  Is cracked by many a space
Of water, flooding its glazed brim:
    In one of these, o weep!
Around the full, soft bosom and soft wings
Of Aphrodite's swan the ice-ridge clings,
    Able to stem his grace,
Deride his whiteness, numb his warmth, and
      make
    A prison of his lake.

    Alas!
  My heart is frozen up with scorn,
    Is broken with neglect,
  And therein Love is left forlorn,
    A soft, banned thing, alas!
That finds no passage it can cleave to hope,
  And for its graciousness no scope
    By cruel frosts uncheckt,
No freedom in the realm where once it moved
    Delightful and beloved.

MY heart is a violin
    This morning as I listen;
For the trill of a bird, though thin,
    Yet a trill in which raindrops glisten
        And sunshine quivers,
    Twangs a chord of my heart
        That sharply cries and shivers
        And hails the smart.

Again my heart-string bears
    The merciless vibration,
As that trill comes unawares
    To incite, and tease with cessation
        When just awaking
    The music into fire :
        O heart, a viol quaking
        With vain desire !

DELICIOUSLY I wake to-day !
    A slave I went to bed,
    But Love is gone away ;
A slave last night, I wake instead
    Free to enjoy and free
To ponder, with no fear that thought

By one rich face shall be
Entangled and distraught.

I wake, and I am free to rove,
    Not wearying to know
    Along what path my love
May at the moment chance to go.
    I can be sad, can cry,
And have no cruel dread meantime
    That he is doomed to die
    In some malignant clime.

Free to the world that once I knew,
    Now from young morning skies
    I shall receive the blue,
Nor make it fashion me his eyes:
    The rose is crimson-rose,
No matter for his lip or cheek;
    And as the river flows
    I do not hear him speak.

And I am bold to breathe and change
    Just as it pleases me,
    So far beyond his range
I set my new philosophy;

I look with honest eyes,
Hear with true ears ; and, best of all,
When tired of being wise,
Again can be Love's thrall.

L EDA was wearied of her state, the crown
      was heavy on her head ;
She put the crown away,
And ran down to the river-bed
For a whole holiday.

She came to draw free, lonely breaths beside
      the mellow, autumn pools ;
Counting their starry drops,
She mused on the lone god who rules
Above the mountain-tops.

And, as she worshipped him with secret heart,
      among the willow-trees
She felt how something sailed
And gathered round her as a breeze :
The breath within her failed.

There were white feathers on her breast when
      she awoke; the water stirred

With motion of white wings,
And in her ear that note she heard
    The swan a-dying sings.

A NIGHTINGALE wakes me. Think of
        this !—
While she sings so loud,
A woman is lying in her shroud
To whom a lover has never vowed :
O wrong in the world, and by God allowed !

Ah me, a girl to be dead, and miss
    That high-and-away, that clang of pain,
    The way Love trebles his sweets again,
    And then feels it vain,
Jar, jarra ! and keeps to the mocking strain !

A S children loosed to summer days
        When dreary tasks are done,
With choral leap and laughter raise
A pæan of undaunted praise
    For golden sunlight won,
So leaps my thought, rejoicing, free,
When the world looses it to thee.

TWO lovers came; of many a common
      thing
   We talked ; then in a ring
Drew toward the hearth ; the winter daylight
      died,
   And she was at his side;
   He took, he stroked her hand
      That we might know
      It is just so
Love loves; the cadence of our talk grew low,
   The fire shot forth a brand.

Then we forgot the lovers; for the room
   Was filling with a doom,
The pressure of a Presence that we felt
   Had power with them that dwelt
   In many a distant land,
      And with the dead.
      No word we said,
But in a stupor watched the firelight shed
   Glow on the fondled hand.

WHEN the fire on the hearth falls into
      embers,
   Then most we love to sit beside the fire :

And thus it comes to pass in dull Novembers
   The poet, feeling blindly for his lyre,
      Breaks with desire
For the rain, the light, the lovely sunshine he
    remembers.

The lover of the forest oftenest chooses
   To walk there when it thinneth tree by tree,
And so it comes to pass, when life refuses
   To give us any more felicity,
      We wander free
To the founts, the wells, the inviolate grots of
    the Muses.

A BALLAD

I N winter, afternoons are short;
  It was a winter afternoon.
The milking was already done;
I took my man, I took my gun,
   That we might have some sport.

We stooped behind the tallest brake:
There was a bush of golden furze;
The furze has scent so rich and full

H

It makes the sense a little dull :
   I hardly felt awake.

Oh, could it be the whirr of game,
That sudden, little spring of noise !
Robin was shouting in the wind ;
He must have left me far behind,
   So faint his whistle came.

I felt the bushes with my hand :
There was a certain furrowed nook—
The gorse with fire was black and brown,
But there the music drew me down
   Into a clear, white land.

There was more grass than I could see,
The grass was marked with pale, green rings ;
And oh, the sudden joy I felt
To see them dancing at full pelt,
   The whole Fair Family.

We did not touch the pale, green rings,
I think we eddied through the air ;
A swirl of dew was in my face,

And, looking downward, I could trace
   The mark of pale, green rings.

The measure scarcely was begun ;
I could have danced a hundred years !
But Robin, he would surely scoff—
Straightway I broke the measure off :
   My eyes blinked in the sun.

If Robin should be come to harm !
I looked for him to left, to right :
In winter, afternoons are short,
It was too late to think of sport ;
   I turned back to the farm.

My mother all the tale should know.
How thick the trees above the hedge !
There was a pond that I must pass ;
I looked in it as in a glass ;
   My hair was white as snow.

The servants saw me pass and smiled.
But that was not the worst, for when
I looked in at the parlour door

The children rose up from the floor :
   I had no wife or child.

They gathered round me in a flock;
The mistress jeered.   But who was he,
That old man with the bald, bent head ?
Oh, he would know I had been dead,
   He would not feel the shock.

His master was away from home,
He said, and rose to give mé food ;
" But my old master has been lost
These fifty years."   A terror crost
   His breast, and he was dumb.

I could not touch the wheaten bread,
So plain I saw the clear, white land.
O cursèd, cursèd elfin-race,
Mid living men I have no place,
   And yet I am not dead.

I travel on from town to town,
But always by a dusty road,
By market-streets, by booths and fairs ;

I have great terror of the snares
  Upon the furzy down.

But I must see my home once more,
Nor fear to eat the wheaten bread.
Oh, some day I must see my friend,
And eat with him, and make an end,
  For Robin is fourscore.

EARLY lambs and hail,
    Winds and nipped, green leaflet :
    Yet, oh 'yet,
Joy that cannot fail
Rises ever faster,
Spite of each disaster.
Perfect leaves and roses
Succeed the starvling posies,
A song-enwoven breeze
Stops March's cruelties.

So Love's every fear,
Crosses and complaining
      Still should bring
Happiness more near,
Fuller-hearted kisses,
And completest blisses.

Love without fruition
Hath marred its living mission,
Hath lost its nature quite—
March with no May delight.

MY love was like a dormant chrysalid
        Which thou didst lay
In thy heart's casket, that it might be hid
        From the cold light away.
Warmly it wintered in its prison-room;
        Thou wouldst not let it die.
            In April bloom
        It opened to an azure butterfly,
With wings that languished for the beds of
        broom,
And the soft joys that come of liberty.
        Thou wouldst not let it free,
            And it lay there
Dead of its fostered yearning's young despair,
        When thou didst lift the lid.

THE lady I have vowed to paint
        Has contour of a rose,

No rigid shadow of a saint
        Upon the wall she throws;
    Her tints so softly lie
Against the air they almost vie
With the sea's outline smooth against the sky.

To those whom damask hues beguile
        Her praise I do not speak,
I find her colour in the smile
        Warm on her warm, blond cheek :
    Then to the eyes away
It spreads, those eyes of mystic gray
That with mirage of their own vision play.

Her hair, about her brow, burns bright,
        Her tresses are the gold
That in a missal keeps the light
        Solemn and pure.   Behold
            Her lashes' glimmerings
Have the dove's secret springs
Of amber sunshine when she spreads her wings.

NOON

FULL summer and at noon; from a waste
        bed

Convolvulus, musk-mallow, poppies spread
The triumph of the sunshine overhead.

Blue on refulgent ash-trees lies the heat ;
It tingles on the hedge-rows ; the young wheat
Sleeps, warm in golden verdure, at my feet.

The pale, sweet grasses of the hayfield blink ;
The heath-moors, as the bees of honey drink,
Suck the deep bosom of the day.   To think

Of all that beauty by the light defined
None shares my vision! Sharply on my mind
Presses the sorrow : fern and flower are blind.

A SHADY silence fills,
    At deep mid-eventide,
The rockless land of hills
    Where two slow rivers glide.
The gnats beneath the gloom
        Have failed in song,
Yet something through the combe
    Comes like a sound along,
Though very far as yet,
    Though no one is in sight,

Nor could a mortal set
Such alien echoes moving through the night.

'Tis not an hour to fear:
    The sun is gone to bed,
The clouds from dusk are clear,
    And there are overhead
But one or two large stars,
        A bat or two.
Yet, hark! a jangle mars
    The peaceful mountain-view,
Like the far cry of hounds
    Chasing a distant prey:
The chime of yelping sounds—
Oh, will it sink, or will it swell this way?

It comes as comes the wind,
    With little noise at first.
Exultantly combined,
    Halloes and bays outburst
Upon that solitude
        Where two streams meet:
Then in a scramble rude
    Of shoulders, ears, and feet

The banhounds rush along,
    And drive before their jaws
A wincing, naked throng
At flight from heated breath and thorny claws.

These are the souls that moan
    Because upon their birth
God's water was not thrown;
    Or those who left the earth
Impenitent, unblessed.
        Now all must fly,
While summer is at rest,
    And, hunted furiously,
Be caught and bitten through
    By dogs of faery-breed,
Sleek creatures, ebon-blue,
With lusting teeth and fore-ordainèd speed.

They scour the mountain side,
    The upland township, then
Skirt the dark valley wide,
    A cloud of dogs and men :
Behind, tall ladies race,
        Each dressed in green,
Each with a smile-lit face
    And presence of a queen,

Who breathe from steely lips,
  Clap when a soul is caught,
And urge, with corded whips,
The stragglers of the pack to fiendish sport.

Their dogs have ceased to whine ;
  The whining doth not cease.
One cannot watch the kine,
  That chew their cud in peace ;
For still the lengthy curs,
    It almost seems,
Phantasmal haunt the firs,
  Haunt the two voiceless streams :
The sprites themselves have ghosts
  That it is hard to lay,
And echoes walk in hosts
Long after the live echoes pass away.

IRISES

IN a vase of gold
  And scarlet, how cold
The flicker of wrinkled grays
In this iris-sheaf ! My eyes fill with wonder

At the tossed, moist light, at the withered
    scales under
  And among the uncertain sprays.

    The wavings of white
    On the cloudy light,
  And the finger-marks of pearl ;
The facets of crystal, the golden feather,
The way that the petals fold over together,
  The way that the buds unfurl !

CYCLAMENS

THEY are terribly white :
    There is snow on the ground,
And a moon on the snow at night ;
The sky is cut by the winter light ;
Yet I, who have all these things in ken,
Am struck to the heart by the chiselled white
  Of this handful of cyclamen.

A VALLEY of oak-trees,
   A streamlet between them
As twisted as these ;
Few mortals have seen them,

Or crossed the low bridge
From oak-ridge to oak-ridge.
Why is there a bridge
Where no one can heed it,
Nor traveller need it,
Small bridge between small oak-trees?

The Dryads have homesteads,
And cousins and neighbours:
A Dryad, who weds
With a Faun, often labours
To reach her own folk
In some far-away oak;
For she loves the old folk
Of the glade where she tarried
Before she was married;
And then on the bridge she treads.

Or one, who with boldness
Is wooed by a satyr,
Her sandals will press
On the boards, with the patter
Of leaves in the wind;
And looking behind,
Half-scared by the wind,

Her face coy and simple
She hides mid her wimple,
And runs in her floating dress.

Thus often and sweetly
The bridge hath united,
Hath helped those who fly,
Hath brought the invited
And sped the late guest.
From east and from west
Pass lover and guest,
While the bridge is unbroken
In the countryside oaken,
And Dryads and Fauns live by.

THE devil is a sinner,
    Ha, la, la—la!
But none can hit him fair;
For who would be the winner,
    Fa, la, la—la!
Ay, who would be the winner,
    When the devil does not care?

THE iris was yellow, the moon was pale,
 In the air it was stiller than snow,
There was even light through the vale,
    But a vaporous sheet
    Clung about my feet,
  And I dared no further go.
I had passed the pond, I could see the stile,
The path was plain for more than a mile,
    Yet I dared no further go.

The iris-beds shone in my face, when, whist!
  A noiseless music began to blow,
A music that moved through the mist,
    That had not begun,
    Would never be done,
  With that music I must go:
And I found myself in the heart of the tune,
Wheeling round to the whirr of the moon,
    With the sheets of mist below.

In my hands how warm were the little hands,
  Strange, little hands that I did not know:
I did not think of the elvan bands,
    Nor of anything
    In that whirling ring—

Here a cock began to crow!
The little hands dropped that had clung so tight,
And I saw again by the pale dawnlight
    The iris-heads in a row.

FEBRUARY

GAY lucidity,
    Not yet sunshine, in the air;
Tingling secrets hidden everywhere,
    Each at watch for each;
    Sap within the hillside beech,
        Not a leaf to see.

    Windy blusterings
Blow at moments and rejoice;
Oftener still the adolescent voice
    Of a single bird
    Somewhere suddenly is heard
        That desires to sing.

I LAY sick in a foreign land;
    And by me, on the right,
A little Love had taken stand,
    Who held up in my sight

A vessel full of injured things—
His shivered bow, his broken wings;
And underneath the pretty strew
Of glistening feathers, half in view,
A broken heart: he held them up
Within the silver-lighted cup
That I might mark each one, then pressed
His little cheek against my chest,
And fell to singing in such wise
He shook the vision from my eyes.

A HOSPITAL GARDEN

FORTH to the sunshine-mottled weather,
  Forth to the whispering breeze
High overhead! Oh, were there ever
  Such happy groves as these!
One may pick up a wood-dove's feather
    Beneath the tall plane-trees.

TO the forest, ho!
    Where the tall deer run,
  We go, we go,
    And every one
Shall bend his duteous bow.

I

To the forest, hey !
Where the green oaks stand,
    We ride away
    A jolly band,
With, ho! for a greenwood day !

A BALLAD

SHE was a royal lady born,
    Who loved a shepherd-lad ;
To bring the smile into his face
    Was all the care she had.

His murderers brought a bloody croók
    To show her of their deed :
She eyed it with a queenly eye ;
    And leapt into the mead.

And there she settled with the lambs,
    And felt their woolly fleece ;
It was their cry among the hills
    That brought her to her peace.

And when at night she folded them,
   Outside the wattle-fold
She took her lute and sang to them
   To keep them from the cold.

She was a happy innocent
   Whom men had sought to spite.
Alack, no sovereign lady lives
   A life of such delight.

For no one crossed her any more,
   Or sought to bend her will;
She watched the ewes at lambing-time,
   And in the winter chill.

And when her flock was scattered far
   One day beside the brook,
The shepherds found that she had died,
   Her arms about her crook.

She had no memories to forget,
   Nor any sins to weep;
O God, that I might be like her,
   And live among the sheep!

TO fields where now the forests fail
    The nightingale comes back,
To the soft footsteps of the wood so clinging
    As if there were for singing
        One track.

The poet, as the nightingale,
    Must haunt the olden track,
Must sing of Love where Love first heard his
        singing,
    Though there 's no bringing
        Love back.

AN ÆOLIAN HARP

DOST thou not hear ? Amid dun, lonely
        hills
Far off a melancholy music shrills,
As for a joy that no fruition fills.

Who live in that far country of the wind ?
The unclaimed hopes, the powers but half-
        divined,
The shy, heroic passions of mankind.

And all are young in those reverberant bands;
None marshalls them, no mellow voice com-
      mands;
They whirl and eddy as the shifting sands.

There, there is ruin, and no ivy clings;
There pass the mourners for untimely things,
There breaks the stricken cry of crownless
      kings.

But ever and anon there spreads a boom
Of wonder through the air, arraigning doom
With ineffectual plaint as from a tomb.

WE were lovers together side by side,
      The terror that we must part
A nightmare before us, until she died
   And I gathered her to my heart.

THE roses wither and die;
    Close brown is the sweet, loose red;
Love dieth not.
The roses wither and die,

But their fragrance is not dead :
> *Love cannot die,*
> *Love dieth not.*

The roses are shrunk and dry ;
On their dimmed rose death is fed ;
Love dieth not.
The roses are shrunk and dry,
Their leaves on the earth are spread :
> *Love cannot die,*
> *Love dieth not.*

The flower on the ground must lie,
The loose, sweet leaves must be shed ;
Love dieth not.
The flower on the ground must lie
To heap up a balsam-bed :
> *Love cannot die,*
> *Love dieth not.*

COME, mete me out my loneliness, o wind,
    For I would know
How far the living who must stay behind
    Are from the dead who go.

Eternal Passer-by, I feel there is
    In thee a stir,
A strength to span the yawning distances
    From her grave-stone to her.

FROM PAUL VERLAINE
"Il pleure dans mon cœur"

THERE are tears in my heart,
    There is rain in the town ;
What bodeth this smart
In my languorous heart ?

O soft noise of the rain
Over earth, on the roof !
For a heart sick with pain
O the song of the rain !

Tears with no reason
In a heart out of heart.
And none has wrought treason?
This grief has no reason.

'Tis indeed the worst woe,
With no love and no hate
In one's heart, not to know
Why one's heart has such woe.

WE meet. I cannot look up; I hear
    He hopes that the rainy fog will clear :
My cheeks flush him back a hope it may,
    And at last I seek his eyes.
    Oh, to greet such skies—
The delicate, violet, thunder gray,
Behind, a spirit at mortal play !
Who cares that the fog should roll away

I HAVE found her power!
    From her roving eyes
    Just a gift of blue,
    That away she threw
As a girl may throw a flower.
    I am weary of glances ;
    This blue enhances
My life : I have found her power.

GREAT violets in the weedy tangle
    Of a corner sunny,
And bees that with the petals wrangle
    For their inmost honey :
Delicate bee-shadows move
    On the old, gray wall,

And the sturdy owners rove
 Thieving one and all.
 O welcome thieves,
 Each heart receives
The prick that takes its bliss !
 O lover-thieves,
No heart would miss
 A visit that bereaves !
 So hearts are made ;
 Sweet violets so
 Are swift waylaid,
 As hive-bees know.

One bee with gracious triumph drunken
 Taps a bud, unwitting
That its sweets are secret, sunken
 From his frenzied hitting ;
He arrives too soon, forsooth,
 With his pain, his fire,
And encounters early youth
 Shut still from desire.
 O Love, not yet
 Your arrows whet !
With tetchy music, see,
 Unloved as yet,

                The thwarted bee
            Flies where he may forget
                His sudden check,
                And meet for hours
                The breath and beck
                Of open flowers.

                ELVAN JUSTICE

THE rooks have their nests above,
        And the rooks we do not love.
The man who will break their eggs
        Shall have half-a-crown
In the midst of the ring, where we twirl our
                legs,
        Laid every morning down,
As white as any he ever saw,
        Or shall ever see.
            Ha, ha, hi, hi!
            Caw, caw!

        The rooks in the happy sun
        Have no bewildering fun,
    No frolic, nor ease, nor dance;
        And are black indeed,

For they talk of affairs, or preach perchance,
      Or blab of what they need.
We hate them because they keep the law,
      And are cold to glee.
            Ha, ha, hi, hi !
            Caw, caw !

   The rooks in the budding elm
   With their requiem overwhelm
Our pipes and our gay, little strings;
      When round and round we go,
And with delicate whizz of our pointed wings
      Ride on the music so.
Reproof is tolled from each deadly maw
      Down the budding tree.
            Ha, ha, hi, hi !
            Caw, caw !

   The rook is a wicked bird,
   By joy it is never stirred;
So the man who loves us best
   And has loved our folk,
Will fling down the eggs from the troublesome
      nest,
   And spill them yolk by yolk,

To stop while there's time each clanking jaw,
    And to set us free.
        Ha, ha, hi, hi!
            Caw, caw!

I WILL sing what happened to-night on
                high:
        In the frank, wide sky
The wind had put the sun to rout,
The tossed west-clouds were floating about;
From the wreath above me, staid and prim,
            A star looked out,
            Preparing to trim
Her lamp, and to shine as she had shined
        Worlds out of mind:
When lo! she felt the wind on her face,
            And for joy of him
            She left the place
            Where she had shined
            Worlds out of mind,
To run through the frank, wide sky:
She was veiled by the clouds a moment or two,
Then I saw her scouring across the blue,
            For joy of the wind.

TRIUMPH OF BACCHUS AND ARIADNE
From LORENZO DI MEDICI
"Quant' è bella giovinezza"

AH, how beautiful is youth,
   Youth that fleets so fast away !
He who would be gay, forsooth,
Let him hasten to be gay !
This is Bacchus we are seeing,
Ariadne—how they glow !
Always happy and agreeing,
Since 'tis plain that nothing matters
While they love each other so ;
And these others, nymphs and satyrs,
Dance beside them all the way :
He who would be gay, forsooth,
Let him hasten to be gay.

See ! these little fauns, a-bubble
With pure mischief, muse and plot
How to get the nymphs in trouble,
And a thousand traps have baited
Mid the bushes, in the grot ;
Now by Bacchus' heat elated
They are skipping all the way :
He who would be gay, forsooth,
Let him hasten to be gay.

And the tricksome nymphs discover
It is nice to be pursued,
Caught and worried by a lover ;
Who should frown at Love's ensnaring
Were a thankless creature rude;
So they mingle, pleasure sharing,
Making gambol all the way :
He who would be gay, forsooth,
Let him hasten to be gay.

On an ass Silenus hoary
Rides, with all his flesh and years,
Drunken, steeped in Bacchic glory.
At his figure's backward swaying
He is foremost in his jeers;
And at whiles, in snatches singing
With the others, cheers the way :
He who would be gay, forsooth,
Let him hasten to be gay.

This is Midas : as they tell us,
All he touches turns to gold,
But his gift scarce makes us jealous ;
For what good is there in treasure,
Treasure more than man can hold,

If he cannot take his pleasure,
Being thirsty all the way?
He who would be gay, forsooth,
Let him hasten to be gay.

Now all ears be set a-tingle,
Open, quick to every bliss!
Young and old together mingle,
Young nor old possess the morrow,
'Tis to-day we meet and kiss;
We must drop our grief, for sorrow
Would pollute this holy way:
He who would be gay, forsooth,
Let him hasten to be gay.

Youth and maiden, swell the chorus!
In our hearts how warm and sweet
Thus to feel the gods are for us,
Loving music, loving dances,
Merry with our moving feet!
Let misfortune as it chances
Strike across us on our way:
He who would be gay, forsooth,
Let him hasten to be gay.
Ah, how beautiful is youth,
Youth that fleets so fast away!

FROM POLIZIANO
"Ciascum segua, o Baccho, te"

ON, o Bacchus, on we go:
  Evoe Bacchus, Bacchus io!
For our heads the ivy-berry
And green ivy-leaf we get,
Serving thee we all make merry,
Nor by night nor day forget
Bacchus in our midst is set.
Drink, and I among you, so:
On, o Bacchus, on we go:
I have drained my horn, delaying
Scarce a moment: put the tun
Nearer.   How this hill is swaying,
Or my brain, has that begun
Spinning circles?   All should run
Up and down as I do, so:
On, o Bacchus, on we go!
Dead with sleep, I stand unsteady:
I am drunk?   But am I?   Nay?
All of you are drunk already,
That I see as clear as day.
Everyone should take my way:
Everyone should stagger, so:
On, o Bacchus, on we go!

Cups we empty without number,
Shouting *Bacchus, Bacchus!* then
Down our bodies drop in slumber.
Drink each one, and drink again.
I shall lead the measure—when ?
For my dance is over.   Io !
On, o Bacchus, on we go :
Evoe Bacchus, Bacchus io !

NOW is youth in season,
     Youth is upmost,
          Youth can boast
Age is but discovered treason,
     That effetely
Yields its place to flowers and boys.
Spring is but a track of joys,
     And completely
Saves from all that chills and cloys.

From the ice's keeping
     Bounds the streamlet,
          Sunny-wet,
With no law to stay its leaping ;

K

Shoots, outrageous,
Stand upon the dead, old leaves;
Grown courageous,
Its dry sheath each leaf-bud cleaves.

Out of nests deep-hidden
Fly the nestlings
On new wings,
Leaving tutelage unbidden
And forever,
Taking through the air such way
As they sever
For themselves by night and day.

Cramping age, be fearful!
Under April
Bow your will;
Be you proud or be you tearful,
Youth is stronger
Than your wail, your frosts or pride,
And no longer
Will your interdict abide.

Yearning boy and maiden,
    Age's trammel
      Is a spell
Ye can break, o duty-laden,
    If hoar rigour
And all gluing bonds ye fight
    With a vigour
That is Life's decisive might.

I WOULD not be a fugitive
  Far in the past amid the olden,
Fond times men labour to recover,
But in the age, ah, verily the golden,
When first a girl dares to become a lover.

How sweeter far it is to give
Than just to rest in the receiving,
Sweeter to sigh than be sighed over,
Sweeter to deal the blow than bear the grieving,
That girl will learn who dares become a lover.

The songs she sings will have the glee,
The laughter of the wind that looses
Wing and breaks from a forest cover;

Freedom of stream that slips its icy nooses
Will be her freedom who becomes a lover.

What Eden unto Eve the tree
Of Life to pluck, to eat unchidden,
Then as a hostess to discover
To man the feast, himself a guest new-bidden,
Now she at last dares to become his lover !

SUNSHINE is calling :
  River-ice grows soft,
  Trees toss the tender leaves aloft
 That frost or sheath were thralling :
O Bacchus, these are drunk with that
Kindling the wine that brims thy autumn vat !

And here are dances
  Underneath the trees,
  As shadow after shadow flees
 With jest and sunny glances :
O Bacchus, these are drunk with that
Kindling the wine that brims thy autumn vat !

The hills, noon-lighted,
  And the shady grove
  Become the purple satyrs love
To quaff, by thirst incited :
O Bacchus, these are drunk with that
Kindling the wine that brims thy autumn vat !

All creatures waken ;
  Warm in dappled grass
  Their gladsome wooing comes to pass ;
Wild love is sought and taken :
O Bacchus, these are drunk with that
Kindling the wine that brims thy autumn vat !

With shout and chorus
  Birds are making joy,
  Their voices have but one employ,
To sing *The woods are for us !*
O Bacchus, these are drunk with that
Kindling the wine that brims thy autumn vat !

The happy breezes
  Sleep with humming breath,
  Then grow so still, it might be death
Their wanton pleasure eases :

O Bacchus, these are drunk with that
Kindling the wine that brims thy autumn vat!

And flowers, sweet-hearted,
   Put away their shame;
   In openness to heaven's flame
The honey-buds have parted:
O Bacchus, these are drunk with that
Kindling the wine that brims thy autumn vat!

Ye women, greet it!
   Light hath called you, come!
   Love, sing, no more be cold and dumb;
Light calls you, meet it!
O women, be ye drunk with that
Kindling the wine that brims the autumn vat!

For light delivers!
   Blood as wine runs red
   When radiance is through it spread,
When with gay spring it quivers:
O Bacchus, be it drunk with that
Kindling the wine that brims thy autumn vat!

O Bacchus, Bacchus,
  Thou without the sun
  Couldst never do what thou hast done,
 Nor with thy fire attack us!
Nay, nay, we only can be drunk with that
Kindling the wine that brims thy autumn vat!

NOTE.

SOME of these Songs and Verses have been collected from the plays in which they found a place, and others are reprinted from the "Contemporary Review," "The Spectator," "The Academy," and the "Scottish Art Review."

CHISWICK PRESS :—C. WHITTINGHAM AND CO.,
TOOKS COURT, CHANCERY LANE.